London can boast of no burial-places that are comparable with Woodlawn and Greenwood; but this is one of the most attractive. It lies upon a side hill. Entering the gateway—guarded by a man in the everlasting gilt-band and buttons—we found the tombs huddled very closely together. One of the first we came to bears the fragrant name of "James Hamilton, D.D., the Beloved Pastor of Regent Square Presbyterian Church." In that grave lies the finest poetic genius that has graced the London pulpit during the present generation. It startled us to discover, a few rods off, the tomb of Tom Sayers the pugilist, with the effigy of a huge stone bull-dog lying beside it! Whose tablet is that one set in yonder wall under the trees? We drew near and read on it the name of Michael Faraday. He was a Sandemanian in his theology; as devout in his faith as he was brilliant in his scientific discoveries. We walked on, under the hot sun, towards the foot of the hill, and came upon a dark granite obelisk about seven feet high, standing amid a small bed of purple flowers. It bore this inscription—"Here lies the body of 'George Eliot' (Mary Ann Cross). Born Nov. 22, 1819—Died Dec. 22, 1882." If the piety of James Hamilton could be combined with the rare genius that wrote Adam Bede and Middlemarch, a splendid ideal would be realized. 1885.

Dag[e] by Kilburn Eng[d] by A H Ritchie

James Hamilton

THE ROYAL PREACHER.

Lectures on Ecclesiastes.

BY

JAMES HAMILTON, D.D., F.L.S.,

AUTHOR OF "LIFE IN EARNEST," "MOUNT OF OLIVES," "HAPPY HOME," "LIFE OF LADY COLQUHOUN," ETC. ETC.

NEW YORK:
ROBERT CARTER & BROTHERS,
No. 285 BROADWAY.

1852.

THOMAS B. SMITH, STEREOTYPER,
216 WILLIAM STREET, N. Y.

ROBERT CRAIGHEAD, PRINTER,
112 FULTON STREET, N. Y.

Contents.

Preface.

In the form of translations, expositions, and literary parallels, there is now connected with each book of the Bible a very extensive authorship; and we might fill a little volume with a historical review of the illustrations of Ecclesiastes, from the Commentary of Jerome to the illuminated edition of Owen Jones.

Jerome tells us that his work originated in an effort to bring over to the monastic life a young Roman lady, Blesilla. This object gives an ascetie tone to every chapter, and many of his interpretations are so fanciful that alongside of them any modern Cocceius would be deemed sober and literal. For instance, applying to the Saviour the language of the second chapter, the "slaves," or men-servants there mentioned, he thinks are Christians afflicted with the spirit of bondage; the "great and small cattle," are the simpletons and drudges of the Church,—its "sheep and oxen," who, without exerting their reason or studying the Scriptures, do as they are bidden, but are not entitled to rank as men, &c. His own reason the learned father freely exercised in his scriptural studies; and he takes care to apprise his readers that his version is the result of his independent research.* For this he has been curiously rewarded. The Council of Trent has declared his version "authentic," and has virtually decreed that henceforth Jerome's private judgment must be the judgment of Christendom. The most painful thing in his writings is the tone of litigious infelicity by which they are pervaded. It is a sort of formic acid which flows from the finger-points not of our good father alone, but of a whole class of Divines; and, like the red marks left by the feet of ants on litmus-paper, it discolors all his pages. But although we cannot sub-

* "Nullius autoritatem secutus sum;" "nec contra conscientiam meam, fonte veritatis omisso, opinionum rivulos consectarer."

scribe to every rendering of the Latin Vulgate, and must demur to its author's principles of interpretation as well as his spirit,—the zeal and industry of Jerome, and the curious information which he has transmitted, must always secure for his name a prominent place in the history of Biblical literature.

To the monk of Bethlehem, we have a curious contrast in Martin Luther. "Fathers and doctors have grievously erred in supposing that in this book Solomon taught contempt of the world, as they call it, meaning thereby contempt of things ordained and created. The creatures are good enough, but it is man and man's notions which Solomon pronounces vanity. But his expounders, forsooth! make it out that the creatures are the vanity, and that they themselves and their dreams are the only solidity! And thus, from the Divine gold of our author they have forged their own abominable idols." And then, in that spirit of genial life-enjoyment with which the "Table Talk" and Merle D'Aubigné's History have made us so familiar, he states it as the true scope of Ecclesiastes: "Solomon wishes to make us tranquil in the ordinary on-goings and accidents of this existence, neither afraid of future days nor covetous of remote possessions;* as St. Paul says, 'careful for nothing.'" And then in a strain very different from that which sought to decoy Blesilla into a convent, and like the uncaged captive, which he really was, the Saxon swan† goes on to celebrate the joys of Christian liberty.

Since that period, versions and commentaries have appeared sufficient to store a little library. In one thing they all agree. They all allow that Ecclesiastes contains many things hard to be understood. "Mea sententia inter omnia sacra scripta liber longe obscurissimus," says Mercer, the learned Hebrew professor in Paris University; "le plus difficile de tous les livres de l'Ecriture," re-echoes his still more learned countryman, Calmet. "Of all the Hebrew writings, none present greater obstacles

* "Sine cura et cupiditate futurorum."

† Luther's crest was a swan, as those will remember who recall the narrative of Huss's Martyrdom.

to the expositor," is the preliminary remark of one of the most intelligent English translators, G. Holden; and even German clairvoyance acknowledges "Finsterniss" and "Dunkelheit." "Zwar hat das Licht der neuern Exegese die dunkle Wolke zertheilt, aber sie doch noch nicht in völlige Klarheit aufgelöst," was the confession of Umbreit thirty years ago, and it is still repeated by most of his critical successors.

There is another respect in which these commentators are all agreed, and in consequence of which their productions remarkably vary. Unconsciously they transfer to their authors their own subjectivity, and Solomon is made to assume a sanguine or atrabilious aspect, or he becomes a poet, a logician, a satirist, or a penitent, according to the mood of his interpreter. As meteorologists employ a cyanometer for ascertaining the depth of azure in the atmosphere, so we once thought of preparing a physiognomic scale, where the academic learning and sober sense of Bishop Patrick might have served as a medium between the dry severity and point-splitting precision of Broughton* at the one extreme, and the good-natured excursiveness and hazy idealism of Greena way† at the other. But remembering how it has fared with the inventors of dangerous instruments, from the days of Lord Morton downwards, we have thought it better to leave oui criticometer incomplete for the present.

Not to enumerate the older works of Desvœux, (1760), L. Holden (1764), and Hodgson (1790), and the well-arranged and scholar-like publication of G. Holden (1822), two very good English translations of Ecclesiastes have lately appeared. Of these, the most elaborate is by the Rev. T. Preston, of Cambridge, and is accompanied by the ingenious Commentary of

* See "The works of the great Albionean Divine renown'd in many nations for rare skill in Salem's and Athens' tongues, and familiar acquaintance with all Rabbinical learning, Mr. Hugh Broughton." London, 1662.

† In Greenaway's curious medley the only unity is indignation, not wholly unmerited, at Houbigant. The very index reads, "Houbigant, tolerable, 190; intolerable, 61; impertinent, *passim;* his spiteful and scandalous attempt to wound the Sacred Text, 67; disgusting, 197; correcting Virgil, 234."

Rabbi Mendlessohn (1845). The other by Dr. Noyes of Boston, U. S. (1846), with less show of erudition, is clear and straightforward; but, like Mendlessohn, the American professor gives to the book an air of theological tenuity, and mere worldly wisdom, which carries neither our conviction nor our sympathy.

In the "Presbyterian Review" (Edinburgh), for October, 1846, there was inserted a brief but interesting paper on this book, ascribed, we believe correctly, to our friend, the Rev. A. A. Bonar. Full of fine fancy and delicate insight, its only fault is its shortness; and although we have taken another view of the book's purport and ground-plan, we could wish that its text were illustrated by a mind so rich in Eastern lore and Christian experience.

Our own labors were nearly ended before there came into our hands the "Biblical Repository" (New York) for April, 1850, containing a Lecture by Professor Stowe, of Cincinnati. The plan of Ecclesiastes, as given by this ingenious expositor, is so nearly akin to that which will be found in the subsequent pages, that we feel bound to transcribe it:— "The method of the writer is the most vivid and effective that can be conceived. Instead of describing the various processes of thought and feeling through which Solomon passed in the course of his eventful life, the whole heart of the king is taken out and held up before our eyes, with everything it contains, both good and bad. The secret chambers of his soul are thrown open, and we see every thought and feeling as it arises in the mind, and in the exact shape in which it first presents itself, without any of those modifications by which men soften down the harder features of their first thoughts before they give them utterance to their fellow-men." "Solomon . . . . seeking happiness in the things of earth, ... is disappointed and disgusted; and instead of repenting of his errors, he becomes dissatisfied with the arrangements of Providence, misanthropic, and skeptical. His conscience, however, is not entirely asleep, but occasionally interposes to check his murmurings and reprove him for his follies. In this state of mind he is introduced, and in the character of Koheleth, gives full and strong utterance to all his feelings. Hence, inconsistent statements and wrong sentiment are to be expected in the progress of the discourse; and it is not till the close of the book that all his errors are corrected, and he comes to 'the conclusion of the whole matter,' a humbled, penitent, believing, religious man."

Of those older commentators who are hortatory rather than explanatory, Reynolds is by far the best. The "Homilies" of Thomas Cartwright, and the "Expositions" of Granger (1621), and Nisbet (1694), contain many pious and useful reflections; but they are not likely to find many modern readers. In our own day, Dr. Wardlaw has published two volumes of Lectures, which are distinguished by richly scriptural illustration and faithful enforcement of truth on the conscience, conveyed in language remarkable for its clearness and elegance, and which promise long to retain a firm hold of the public mind.

Two poetical paraphrases of Ecclesiastes have been written by authors whose opposite fortunes are striking illustrations of their theme. One is entitled, "The Design of Part of the Book of Ecclesiastes: or, the Unreasonableness of Men's Restless Contentions for the Present Enjoyments, represented in an English Poem."* It was the maiden effort of William Wollaston, afterwards sufficiently known through "The Religion of Nature Delineated." He published it in all the gaiety of his spirits, when, from being an ill-paid schoolmaster, he found himself suddenly the heir of a rich kinsman, and when with his newly-married wife, also an heiress, he had settled in a handsome

* London, 1691. It is anonymous; but the Preface is signed "W. W." It is now very rare. The author afterwards wished to suppress it. See Biogr. Brit. 4304.

Amongst other bibliographical curiosities connected with this portion of Scripture may be mentioned, "King Solomon his Solace. Containing (among many thinges of right worthy request) King Solomon his Politie, his true Repentance, and finally his Salvation. [By John Carpenter.] London, 1606." It is a dialogue between Zadoc and Solomon's chief lords, filling a black-letter quarto. It is quaint and ingenious; but owing to its tediousness, its rarity is neither to be wondered at nor regretted.

house, and surrounded himself with a splendid library in Charter House-square. The other is "Choheleth; or, the Royal Preacher, a Poetical Paraphrase of the Book of Ecclesiastes; printed for J. Wallis, at Yorick's Head, Ludgate-street, 1768." It was probably written within a few yards of Wollaston's former mansion; for its author died a pensioner in the Charter House, January, 1795, aged eighty-eight years. "He was at the time of the earthquake a considerable merchant at Lisbon, and narrowly escaped with his life, after seeing all his property swallowed up. Some time after his arrival in England he lost his eyesight, when Her Majesty was pleased to give him her warrant for the comfortable asylum he enjoyed till his death. He was well versed in different languages, and was the author of several detached publications."* What an example of

* From a MS. note appended to our copy of "Choheleth." We have not been able to find any notice of Brodick in print. His paraphrase was reprinted at Whitchurch, Salop (1824), "With Supplementary Notes, by Nathaniel Higgins;" but the editor does not appear to have known even the name of his author.

the "time to get and the time to lose!" The fagged schoolmaster transformed in a few months into the full-blown gentleman, and admitted to courtly circles with his beautiful heiress; and the prosperous merchant seeing his wealth in a moment engulfed by the earth whence it came, and then losing the eyes that beheld it, and thankful for a home in a public hospital! Brodick's Paraphrase indicates considerable poetical talent, and, although too copious, it is so good a transfusion of the original that the Commentary of the learned Dr. Clarke in a great measure consists of extracts from it. On the score of neither versification nor fidelity is Wollaston's poem entitled to equal praise; and by treating Solomon as a satirist he has evidently misapprehended his character; but as the book is now seldom seen, we may give a short sample of the opening chapter:—

"Here Mocher bustles in a thronged shop,
That swallows all his hours to feed his hope;
And pants, by business elbow'd every way,
Within the narrow limits of the day.

There sails a Tyrian by some distant star,
Bolder than fits of men in deep despair :
While Iccar keeps within his native sphere,
Always at home, yet, too, a traveller :
For daily tramping o'er his spacious fields,
He views their state, and what each of them yields;
O'erlooks his flocks, o'erlooks his men, that plough,
Or (his own emblem) corn and fodder mow;
While sweat, the curse, that vanquish'd all our race,
In pearly drops does triumph on his face.

But Oh, that here the catalogue might close!
For still worse ends men to themselves propose;
And still worse roads to reach their goals they choose.
Methinks I see the crafty Gilonite,
Broke from the cords of duty and of right,
Within his study (forge of treasons) sit,
And scratching prompt his head and stir his wit,
Seeking through policy and state essays
Himself, tho' by his master's fall, to raise.
While Absalom (what pity 't should be he!)
The fairest youth e'er blotted family,
A more compendious rebel strives to be;
Through David's and his father's breast would bore
A purple passage to the sovereign power."

An effort of a much higher order than either of the above is Prior's "Solomon." However, being neither a paraphrase nor an independent poem, but a monologue composed of materials which Ecclesiastes supplies, wit, learning, and melodious verse fail to sustain the interest of the huge soliloquy through its three successive books. And we are inclined to think that the spirit of our author has been as happily caught and his design as successfully carried out by sundry productions which neither profess to translate nor to imitate him. Among these literary parallels we would name Johnson's "Vanity of Human Wishes;" Hannah More's "Search after Happiness;" and Tennyson's "Two Voices;" and above all, "Rasselas."* May we not add the sadly beautiful "Consolatio Philosophiæ," in which the last of the Romans has given us everything except the grand conclusion?

Having gone over two books of the New Testament, the author selected Ecclesiastes as the subject of a congregational lecture. He chose it because it is a book of the Old Testament, and because it is peculiarly adapted to

* "The first sentence of Rasselas would serve equally well as an introduction to Ecclesiastes: 'Ye who listen with credulity to the whispers of fancy, and pursue with eagerness the phantoms of hope: who expect that age will perform the promises of youth, and that the deficiencies of the present day will be supplied by the morrow, attend,' " &c.—Prof Stowe.

the present wistful and restless times. He also hoped that its illustration might promote, especially among the younger members of his flock, the intelligent and expectant study of the sacred Scriptures. With a similar hope he now publishes a portion of these lectures.* The space which it would occupy has compelled him to forego any attempt at detailed exposition, and he has felt constrained to omit many important texts; but he trusts that the friendly reader may be able to glean a few of the Royal Preacher's lessons from the following fragments; and he is sure that in gratitude for brevity every reader will forgive an occasional abruptness. And, although he cannot claim the attention of the theologian, yet he trusts that the following hint may assist some readers who, revering the Word of God, regret that they peruse it with little zest or imperfect understanding.

One pleasant use of a preface is that it enables a writer to record his obligations. To

* The series extended to forty discourses, of which the half are now published, most of them somewhat condensed.

his learned co-presbyter, Professor Lorimer, the author is indebted for the use of many German commentaries, some of which were unknown to him even by name. To his kind friend, Sir William J. Hooker, he sent an inquiry on behalf of the artist who designed the accompanying vignette, and received an answer which will be read with much interest by students of Bible botany:—"I have thought much and read what botanists have written on the 'lily' of Matt. vi. 28; as I have lately been reading a learned dissertation on the mustard-seed of Scripture. But I grieve to say, the more I read on such subjects the more I doubt the possibility of coming to *satisfactory* conclusions on such points. They may amuse the understanding, but cannot convince the judgment. I remember at one time being *satisfied* that the *Amaryllis lutea* was the lily of Scripture. I think Sir J. Smith first maintained *that*, in his pamphlets entitled, 'Considerations respecting Cambridge,' and 'Defence of the Church,' &c., and in 'Flora Græca,' vol. iv. p. 10, where he says:—'Hæc (*Am lutea*) est apud

Atticos planta coronaria, et etiam ad Turcorum sepulchra, amoris ac pietatis causâ, frequentius plantatur, Flores ejus, splendore aureo et verè regali, campos varios Europæ, sole fervidiori illustratos, messe peractâ, pulcherrimè ornant. Hinc liliis agrestibus Evangelii, longe melius quàm lilia candida hortorum, nunquam in Syriâ sponte crescentia, proculdubiò respondent; quod nomine Græco ('Ἄγριο κρίνα ἢ Ἄγριο λαλες, potius λαλος, hodiè) confirmatur.' Kirby replied to this in a little dissertation, published in the "Christian Remembrancer," 1819, or thereabouts. He knocks this pretty hypothesis on the head, by saying this plant could not be used for *fuel*,—and that our Saviour 'begins his exhortation with an emphatical word (καταμαθετε), which enjoins particular attention to an object so as to know it well, implying that an individual must be studied,' &c. Thus he gives his verdict in favor of *Lilium candidum* (not *L. Martagon**), the κρινον of Dioscorides, the withered stems of which are very

* "L. Martagon is rather a northern plant—middle of Europe and Siberia."

likely to be 'cast into the oven.' Smith had maintained that this was not a native of Palestine:—but it is clearly ascertained to be so, and of several parts of Syria, Persia, &c. Were a similar comparison to be drawn in our country at the present day, how would a commentator 1800 years hence, determine what was *the 'Lily'* alluded to,—a term applied to a hundred kinds, varying in beauty, and other qualifications, from the magnificent 'Victoria Water-Lily' to the humble 'Lily of the valley?' In the case in question, I rather agree with Kirby, than with Smith, and the former has brought more learning to bear on the subject."

LECTURE I.

The Preacher.

"I the Preacher was King over Israel in Jerusalem."—
ECCLES. i. 12.

THERE is no season of the year so exquisite as the first full burst of Summer: when east winds lose their venom, and the firmament its April fickleness; when the trees have unreefed their foliage, and under them the turf is tender; when, before going to sleep, the blackbird wakes the nightingale, and night itself is only a softer day; when the dog-star has not withered a single flower, nor the mower's scythe touched one; but all is youth and freshness, novelty and hope—as if our very earth had become a bud, of which only another Eden could be the blossom—as if, with all her green canvass spread, our island were an argosie, floating over seas of balm to some bright Sabbatic haven on the shores of Immortality.

With the Hebrew commonwealth, it was the month of June. Over all the Holy Land there rested a blissful serenity—the calm which follows when successful war is crowned with conquest—a calm which was only stirred by the proud joy of possession, and then hallowed and intensified again by the sense of Jehovah's favor. And amidst this calm the monarch was enshrined, at once its source and its symbol. In the morning he held his levée in his splendid Basilica—a pillared hall a hundred cubits long.* As he sate aloft on his lion-guarded throne, he received petitions and heard appeals, and astonished his subjects by astute decisions and weighty apophthegms, till every case was disposed of, and the toils of kingcraft ended. Meanwhile, his chariot was waiting in the square; and, with disdainful hoofs, the light coursers pawed the pavement, impatient

* See 1 Kings vii.. Josephus' Antiquities, Bk. viii. chaps. 5–7; and Fergusson's "Palaces of Nineveh Restored," (1851,) pp. 225–232.

for their master; whilst, drawn up on either side, purple squadrons held the ground, and their champing chargers tossed from their flowing manes a dust of gold. And now, a stir in the crowd—the straining of necks and the jingle of horse-gear announce the acme of expectation; and, preceded by the tall panoply of the commander-in-chief, and followed by a dazzling retinue, there emerges from the palace, and there ascends the chariot, a noble form, arrayed in white and in silver, and crowned with a golden coronet; and the welkin rings, "God save the King;" for this is Solomon in all his glory. And, as through the Bethlehem gate, and adown the level causeway, the bickering chariot speeds, the vines on either side of the valley give a good smell, and it is a noble sight to look back to yon marble fane and princely mansions which rear their snowy cliffs over the capital's new ramparts. It is a noble sight, this rural comfort and that civic opulence—for they evince the abundance of peace and the abundance of righteousness. And when, through orchards and corn-fields, the progress ends, the shouting concourse of the capital is exchanged for the delights of an elysian hermitage. After visiting his far-come favorites—the "apes and the peacocks,"—the bright birds and curious quadrupeds which share his retirement; after wandering along the terraces, where under the ripening pomegranates roses of Sharon blossom, and watching the ponds where fishes bask amid the water-lilies,—we can imagine him retiring from the sunshine into that grotto which fed these reservoirs from its fountain sealed; or in the spacious parlor, whose fluttering lattice cooled, and whose cedar wainscot embalmed the flowing summer, sitting down to indite a poem, in which celestial love should overmaster and replace the earthly passion which supplied its imagery. Dipping his pen by turns in Heaven's rainbow, and in the prismatic depths of his own felicity, with joy's own ink this Prince of Peace inscribed that Song of Songs which is Solomon's.

It was June in Hebrew history—the top-tide of a nation's happiness. Sitting, like an empress, between the Eastern and Western oceans, the navies of three continents poured their treasures at her feet; and, awed by her commanding name, the dromedaries of Midian and Ephah brought spontaneous tributes of spice, and silver, and precious stones. To build her palaces, the shaggy brows of Lebanon had been scalped of their cedars, and Ophir had bled its richest gold. At the magical voice of the Sovereign, fountains native to distant hills, rippled down the slopes of Zion; and miraculous cities, like Palmyra, started up from the sandy waste. And whilst peace, and commerce, and the law's protection, made gold like brass, and silver shekels like stones of the street, Palestine was a halcyon-nest suspended betwixt the calm wave and the warm sky; Jerusalem was a royal infant, whose silken cradle soft winds rock high up on a castle tower: all was serene magnificence and opulent security.

Just as the aloe shoots, and in one stately blossom pours forth the life which has been calmly collecting for a century, so would it appear as if nations were destined to pour forth their accumulated qualities in some characteristic man, and then they droop away. Macedonia blossomed, and Alexander was the flower of Greece; fiery and effeminate, voluptuous in his valor, and full of chivalrous relentings amidst his wild revenge. Rome shot up in a spike of glory, and revealed Augustus —so stern and so sumptuous, so vast in his conceptions, so unquailing in his projects, so fearless of the world, and so fond of the seven-hilled city—the Imperial nest-builder. Mediæval, martial Europe blossomed, and Godfrey and Richard were the twin-flowers of chivalry—Godfrey the captor of Rome and King of Jerusalem; Richard of the lion-heart, Richard of the hammer-hand. And modern France developed in one Frenchman, the concentration of a people vain and ambitious, restless and rapid, brilliant in sentiment, and brave in battle; and having flowered the fated once, the Gallic aloe can yield no more Napoleons. So with Palestine at the time we speak of. Half-way between the call of Abraham and the final capture of Jerusalem, it was the high summer of Jewish story, and Hebrew mind unfolded in this pre-eminent Hebrew. Full of sublime devotion, equally full of practical sagacity; the extemporizer of the loftiest litany in existence, withal the author of the pungent Proverbs; able to mount up on Rapture's ethereal pinion to the region of the seraphim, but keenly alive to all the details of business, and shrewd in his human intercourse; zealous in collecting gold, yet lavish in expending it; sumptuous in his tastes, and splendid in costume; and, except in so far as intellectual vastitude necessitated a certain catholicity—the patriot intense, the Israelite indeed: like a Colossus on a mountain-top, his sunward side was the glory toward which one Millennium of his nation had all along been climbing,—his darker side, with its overlapping beams, is still the mightiest object in that nation's memory.

You have seen a blight in summer. The sky is overcast, and yet there are no clouds; nothing but a dry and stifling obscuration—as if the mouth of some pestilent volcano had opened, or as if sulphur mingled with the sunbeams. "The beasts groan; the cattle are oppressed." From the trees the embryo fruits and the remaining blossoms fall in an unnoticed shower, and the foliage curls and crumples. And whilst creation looks disconsolate, in the hedgerows the heavy moths begin to flutter, and ominous owlets cry from the ruin. Such a blight came over the Hebrew summer. By every calculation it ought to have been high noon; but the sun no longer smiled on Israel's dial. There was a dark discomfort in the air. The people murmured. The monarch wheeled along with greater pomp than ever; but the popular prince had soured into the despot, and the crown sat defiant on his moody brow; and stiff were the obeisances, heartless the hosannas, which hailed him as he passed. The ways of Zion mourned; and whilst grass was sprouting in the temple-courts, mysterious groves and impious shrines were rising everywhere: and whilst lust defiled the palace, Chemosh and Ashtaroth, and other Gentile abominations, defiled the Holy Land.

And in the disastrous eclipse, beasts of the forest crept abroad. From his lurking-place in Egypt Hadad ventured out, and became a life-long torment to the God-forsaken monarch. And Rezon pounced on Damascus, and made Syria his own. And from the pagan palaces of Thebes and Memphis harsh cries were heard ever and anon, Pharaoh and Jeroboam taking counsel together, screeching forth their threatenings, and hooting insults, at which Solomon could laugh no longer. For amidst all the gloom and misery a message comes from God: the kingdom is rent; and whilst Solomon's successor will only have a fag-end and a fragment, by right Divine ten tribes are handed over to a rebel and a runaway.

What led to Solomon's apostasy? And what, again, was the ulterior effect of that apostasy on himself? As to the origin of his apostasy the Word of God is explicit. He did not obey his own maxim. He ceased to rejoice with the wife of his youth; and loving many strangers, they drew his heart away from God. Luxury and sinful attachments made him an idolater, and idolatry made him yet more licentious: until, in the lazy enervation and languid day-dreaming of the Sybarite, he lost the perspicacity of the sage, and the prowess of the sovereign; and when he woke up from the tipsy swoon, and out of the swine-trough picked his tarnished diadem, he woke to find his faculties, once so clear and limpid, all perturbed, his strenuous reason paralyzed, and his healthful fancy poisoned. He woke to find the world grown hollow, and himself grown old. He woke to see the sun bedarkened in Israel's sky, and a special gloom encompassing himself. He woke to recognize all round a sadder sight than winter—a blasted summer. Like a deluded Samson starting from his slumber, he felt for that noted wisdom which signalized his Nazarite days; but its locks were shorn; and, cross and self-disgusted, wretched and guilty, he woke up to the discovery which awaits the sated sensualist; he found that when the beast gets the better of the man, the man is cast off by God. And like one who falls asleep amidst the lights and music of an orchestra, and who awakes amidst empty benches and tattered programmes —like a man who falls asleep in a flower-garden, and who opens his eyes on a bald and locust-blackened wilderness,—the life, the loveliness, was vanished, and all the remaining spirit of the mighty Solomon yawned forth that verdict of the tired voluptuary:—"Vanity of vanities! vanity of vanities! all is vanity!"

LECTURE II.

The Sermon.

"The words of the Preacher, the son of David, King of Jerusalem. Vanity of vanities, saith the Preacher, vanity of vanities; all is vanity."—ECCLES. i. 1, 2.

THERE are some books of the Bible which can only be read with thorough profit, when once you have found the key. Luther some where tells us, that he used to be greatly damped by an expression in the outset of the Epistle to the Romans. The apostle says, "I am not ashamed of the Gospel; for therein is the righteousness of God revealed." By "righteousness" Luther understood the justice of God—his attributes of moral rectitude; and so understanding it, he could scarcely see the superiority of the Gospel over the Law, and at all events, his troubled conscience could find no comfort in it. But when at last it was revealed to him that the term here alludes not to an attribute of God, but to the atonement of Immanuel—that it means not justice, but God's justifying righteousness—the righteousness which God incarnate wrought out, and which is imputed to the sinner believing—the whole epistle was lit up with a joyful illumination; and the context, and many other passages which used to look so dark and hostile, at once "leaped up and fondled" him with friendly recognition: and to Luther ever after the Gospel was glorious as the revelation and the vehicle to the sinner of a righteousness Divine. To take another instance: many read the Book of Job as if every verse were equally the utterance of Jehovah; and they quote the sayings of Bildad and Zophar as the mind of the Most High; entirely forgetting the avowed structure of the book—forgetting that through five-and-thirty chapters the several collocutors are permitted to reason and wrangle, and "darken counsel by words without knowledge," in order to make the contrast more striking, when at last Jehovah breaks silence and vindicates his own procedure. But when you advert to its real structure—when you group the different elements of its poetic painting—when, under the canopy of a dark cloud, you see the patriarch cowering, and his three friends assailing him with calumnious explanations of his sore affliction; but above that cloud you see Jehovah listening to his loyal servant, and to his pious, but narrow-minded neighbors—listening with a look of fatherly fondness, and from heaven's cornucopia* ready to shower on his servant's head the most overwhelming of vindications—the blessings twice repeated, which Satan snatched away: when you see this, and when you know that Jehovah is to be the last speaker, instead of nervously striving to torture into truths the mistakes of Bildad and Zophar, and of Job himself, you feel that their mistakes are as natural and as needful to the plan of the book, as are all the cross-purposes and contradictory colloquies of a well-constructed drama. And

* Job. xlii. 14, Keren-happuch; *i. e.*, Horn of Plenty.

when so understood, you feel that all the rather because of the misconceptions of the human speakers, the book is eloquent with Divine vindication, and teaches what Cowper sings so touchingly:—

" Ye fearful saints, fresh courage take!
The clouds ye so much dread
Are big with mercy, and shall break
In blessings on your head.

" Blind unbelief is sure to err,
And scan his work in vain;
God is his own interpreter,
And he will make it plain."

Perhaps no portion of Holy Writ more needs a key than the subject of our lecture. On the one hand, Ecclesiastes has always been a favorite book with Infidels. It was a manual with that coarse scoffer, Frederick the Great of Prussia; and both Volney and Voltaire appeal to it in support of their skeptical philosophy. Nor can it be denied that it contains many sentiments at seeming variance with the general purport of the Word of God. "Be not righteous overmuch; why shouldst thou destroy thyself?" "All things come alike to all: there is one event to the righteous and to the wicked; to him that sacrificeth, and to him that sacrificeth not." "There is a time for everything. What profit hath he that worketh in that wherein he laboreth?" "As the beast dieth, so dieth man. Do not both go to one place?" "A man hath no better thing than to eat and drink and be merry." These texts, and many like them, are quoted by the moralists of expediency; by the fatalist, the materialist, the Pyrrhonist, the epicure.

On the other hand, many able commentators have labored hard to harmonize such passages with the sayings of Scripture; I may add, they have labored hard to harmonize them with other sayings of Solomon, and other passages of this self-same book. But I cannot help thinking they have labored in vain. For the moment, and when reading or listening to some eloquent exposition, you may persuade yourself that such texts are, after all, only peculiar and paradoxical ways of putting important truths; but when Procrustes has withdrawn his pressure, and the reluctant sentence has escaped from the screw and lever, it bounds up elastic, and looks as strange and ungainly as ever. Therefore, others have met the difficulty by suggesting that, like Canticles, Ecclesiastes is a dialogue; and into the mouth of an imaginary objector, they put every sentiment which they deem unsuitable to an inspired penman. For such interpellations, however, there is no foundation in the context, where nothing is more obvious than the continuous identity of the speaker; and like another exegetical stratagem which would invert the meaning of such passages by turning them into interrogatories, you feel that it is a clever evasion rather than a conclusive solution.* You would prefer a straightforward exposition which would maintain the unity of the book and the analogy of Scripture, whilst it took the words as they stand.

* As specimens of the interrogatory subterfuge, the reader may compare with the original or with the authorized version the following :—"Shall there then be no remembrance of past or future events? Shall there be no memorial of them among those who shall come after us?"—i. 11. "For cannot that which is crooked be made straight? Cannot that which

This is the sentence with which Ecclesiastes closes: "Let us hear the conclusion of the whole matter: Fear God, and keep his commandments: for this is the whole duty of man. For God shall bring every work into judgment, with every secret thing, whether it be good, or whether it be evil." This is the conclusion of the matter, and a wise and wholesome conclusion, worthy of Him who said, "Seek first the kingdom of God and his righteousness, and all these things shall be added unto you." But what is the "matter" of which this is the "conclusion?" To ascertain this we must go back to the beginning. There you read, "I the preacher was king in Jerusalem, and I gave my heart to search out by wisdom concerning all things that are done under heaven. Then I said in my heart, Go to now, I will prove thee with mirth: therefore enjoy

is wanting be supplied?"—i. 15. "Shall I therefore hate life, because anything wrought under the sun becomes a grievance unto me? Shall I hate my labor which I take under the sun, because I must some time leave it to the man who shall succeed me?"—ii. 17, 18. (*Barham's Corrected Translation.*) Surely the sense is too feeble to justify such a forced construction.

pleasure," &c. In other words, you find that this "matter" was a long experiment, which the narrator made in search of the Supreme Felicity, and of which Ecclesiastes records the successive stages. But how does it record them? By virtually repeating them. In the exercise of his poetic power the historian conveys himself and his reader back into those days of vanity, and feels anew all that he felt then: so that, in the course of his rapid monologue, he stands before us, by turns the man of science and the man of pleasure, the fatalist, the materialist, the skeptic, the epicurean, and the stoic, with a few earnest and enlightened interludes; till, in the conclusion of the whole matter, he sloughs the last of all these "lying vanities," and emerges to our view, the noblest style of man, the believer and the penitent.

This we believe to be the true idea of the book. We would describe it as a dramatic biography, in which Solomon not only records but re-enacts the successive scenes of his search after happiness; a descriptive memoir, in which he not only recites his past experience, but in his improvizing fervor becomes the various phases of his former self once more. He is a restored backslider, and for the benefit of his son and his subjects, and, under the guidance of God's Spirit, for the benefit of the Church, he writes this prodigal's progress. He is a returned pilgrim from the land of Nod, and as he opens the portfolio of sketches which he took before his eyes were turned away from viewing vanity, he accompanies them with lively and realizing repetitions of what he felt and thought during those wild and joyless days. Our great Edmund Burke once said that his own life might be best divided into "fyttes" or "manias:" that his life began with a fit poetical, followed by a fit metaphysical, and that again by a fit rhetorical; that he once had a mania for statesmanship, and that this again had subsided into the mania of philosophical seclusion. And so in his days of apostasy, the soul intense of Solomon launched out into a fit of study, succeeded by a fit of luxury. He had fits of grossness and refinement, a mania of conviviality, a mania of misanthropy. He had a fit of building, a fit of science, a fit of book-making; and they all passed off in collapses of disappointment and paroxysms of downright misery. And here, as he exhibits these successive *tableaux*, these facsimiles of his former self, like a modern lyrist on St. Cecilia's day, he runs the diapason of departed passion, and, in the successive strophes and antistrophes, he feels his former frenzies over again, in order that, by the very vividness of the representation, we may be all the better "admonished."*

"The preacher was king over Israel, and, because he was wise, he taught the people knowledge. He sought to find out acceptable words, and that which was written was upright,"† a true story, a real statement of the case. "And by these, my son, be admonished." 'Do you, my son, accept this father's legacy; and do you, my people, receive at your monarch's hand this "Basilicon Doron," this autobiography of your penitent prince. These chapters are "words of truth; revivals

* Chap. xii. 12. † Chap. i. 12; xii. 9, 10.

of my former self—reproductions of my reasonings and regrets—my fantastic hopes and blank failures, during that sad voyage round the coasts of vanity. "By these be admonished." Without repeating the guilty experiment, learn the painful result—listen to the moans of a melancholy worldling; for I shall sing again some of those doleful ditties for which I exchanged the songs of Zion. Look at these portraits—they are not fancy sketches—they are my former self, or rather, my former selves: that lay figure in the royal robes, surmounted first by the lantern-jaws of the book-worm, now exchanged for the jolly visage of the gay *gourmand*, and presently refining into the glossy locks and languid smile of the Hebrew exquisite: now chuckling with the merriment of the laughing philosopher, curling anon into the bitter sneer of the Cynic, and each in succession exploding in smoke; not a masque, not a mummery; not a series of make-believers, but each a genuine evolution of the various Solomon—look at these pictures, ye worldlings, and as in water face answers to face, so in one or other of these recognize your present likeness and foresee your destiny.'

"All Scripture is given by inspiration of God," and it is not the less "profitable" because some of it is the inspired record of human infirmity. The seventy-third Psalm is a lesser Ecclesiastes. There Asaph tells us the workings of his mind when he saw the prosperity of the wicked. "Behold, these are the ungodly, who prosper in the world. Verily, I have cleansed my heart in vain, and washed my hands in innocency." And he was so full of resentment and envy that his "feet were almost gone." He had "well nigh slipped" into utter apostasy: when a timely visit to the sanctuary intercepted his fall. There two forgotten verities flashed upon his mind:—the coming retribution, and the all-sufficiency of the believer's portion. "Nevertheless, I am continually with thee: thou hast holden me by my right hand. Thou shalt guide me with thy counsel, and afterward receive me to glory. Whom have I in heaven but thee? and there is none upon earth that I desire beside thee.

My flesh and my heart faileth: but God is the strength of my heart, and my portion forever. For lo, they that are far from thee shall perish: thou hast destroyed all them that go a-whoring from thee. But it is good for me to draw near to God: I have put my trust in the Lord God, that I may declare all thy works." And just as Asaph's heart for a time was "grieved,"—"So foolish was I, and ignorant: I was as a beast before thee,"—so Solomon's feet actually slipped, and in this book he gives us his various reasonings whilst still a backslider. And just as Asaph's "conclusion of the whole matter" was the blessedness of piety and the certainty of righteous retribution,—"It is good for me to draw near to God: they that are far from thee shall perish,"—so Solomon's conclusion is identical; "Fear God, and keep his commandments: for this is the whole of man. For God shall bring every work into judgment, with every secret thing, whether it be good, or whether it be evil." It need, therefore, in no wise surprise us if we find in these chapters many strange questionings and startling opinions, before we arrive at the final conclusion. Intermingled with much that is noble and holy, these "doubtful disputations" are not the dialogue of a believer and an infidel, but the soliloquy of a "divided heart"—the debate of a truant will with an upbraiding conscience. As we listen to the inward colloquy we could sometimes fancy that we hear a worldling and a skeptic contending with an Abdiel. But, after all, it is only the fitful meditation of one who once knew better, and who, by bitter discipline, is learning anew the lesson of his youth. We know not to what better to compare it than a labyrinthine journey underground. Impatient of the daylight—quitting those pastures green and paths of righteousness in which he had walked with his saintly sire—tired of religion and its simple pleasures, he dives into a subterranean avenue which is to end in a Goshen of central light—a poet's paradise with emerald turf and flaming flowers. And the first portion of his fantastic path is lighted by radiance from the entrance—the re-collected knowledge of his wiser days.

But that dim twilight fades, and the explorer quickly finds that even Solomon is not phosphorescent, and, stumbling on, he souses into a fetid quag. Struggling through the slough of sensuality, he reaches a brilliant cave, where stalactites of crystal glorify the beams transmitted through the fissured roof, and where the very stones are musical; and, for a season, the royal pilgrim expatiates in a temple sacred to architecture and each fine art. But, wearied with its splendor, shivering at its frosty elegance, he presses on again; and, except when now and then a shaft overhead lets down some light into the dreary tunnel, all benighted,—as on the rugged roof he strikes his brow, or on the flinty splinters wounds his feet,—we can overhear the muffled voice which execrates the vexation and the vanity. And when, at last, with sullied robes and grisled locks he emerges to the spot from which he started, he grudges so long a journey, and a route so painful, back to his better self; and, resuming his old position, though scarcely regaining his original cheerfulness, he advises us to be content with his experiment and to begin with his "conclusion." If, therefore, we remember the real structure of the book, and as a lamp to its dim passages take the light from its final landing-place, much of its obscurity will flee away; and we may listen without disquiet to the darkest queries and most desperate declarations of Solomon benighted, when in Solomon recovered we expect the answer and the antidote.

There is little difference in men's bodily stature. A fathom, or thereabouts—a little more or a little less—is the ordinary elevation of the human family. Should a man add a cubit to this stature, he is followed along the streets as a prodigy; should he fall very far short of it, people pay money for a sight of him, as a great curiosity. But, were there any exact measurement of mental statures, we should be struck by an amazing diversity. We should find pigmy intellects too frequent to be curiosities. We should find fragile understandings to which the grasshopper is a burden, and dwarfish capacities unable to grapple with the easiest problems: whilst, on the other hand, we should encounter a few colossal minds, of which the altitude must be taken not in feet, but in furlongs—tall, culminating minds, which command the entire tract of existing knowledge—minds whose horizon is their coeval hemisphere; or, loftier still, prophetic minds, on which is already shining the unrisen sun of some future century.

Such a mind was Solomon's. His information was vast. He was the Encyclopædia of that early age. He was an adept in the natural sciences:—"He spake of trees, from the cedar to the hyssop; he spake also of beasts, and of fowl, and of creeping things, and of fishes," as the sacred historian simply words it; or, in modern terminology, he was a botanist, and acquainted with all departments of zoology, from the annelida up to the higher vertebrata. His wisdom excelled the wisdom of all the children of the East country, and all the children of Egypt. And then his originality was equal to his information. He was a poet: his "Songs" were upwards of a thousand. And a moralist: his proverbs were three thousand. He was a sagacious politician; and as the chief magistrate of his own empire, he was famous for the equity and acuteness of his decisions. He had a splendid taste in architecture and landscape-gardening; and his enormous wealth enabled him to conjure into palpable realities the visions of his gorgeous imagination; whilst, to crown the whole—unlike Moses and many others, men of stately intellect, but stammering speech—the wisdom of Solomon found utterance in language like itself; and whilst the eloquence still lived of which the Bible has preserved some examples, crowned students and royal disciples came from the utmost parts of the earth to hear the wisdom of Solomon.

Now, this man, so mightily endowed; if you add to his intellectual elevation the pedestal of his rare good fortune, mounting the genius of the sage on the throne of the sovereign—this peerless man, this prime specimen of humanity—it would appear that Providence raised up, for this, among other purposes. From the day when Adam fell it had been the great inquiry among men, Where and how to find the true felicity? And though the Most High assured them that they could only find it where they had formerly enjoyed it—in unison with Himself, and in his conscious friendship: of this they were quite incredulous. It was still the problem, Apart from infinite excellence, how shall we be happy? Though blessedness was not far from any one of them, in delirious search of it, men burrowed in gold mines, and rummaged in the rubbish-heaps, drilled deep into the rock, and dived deep into the sea. And though none succeeded, few despaired. There was always an apology for failure. They had sought in the right direction, but with inadequate appliances. They were not rich enough; they were not strong enough; they were not clever enough. Had they been only a little wealthier; had they been better educated; had they possessed more leisure, talent, power—they were just about to touch the talisman: they would have brought to light the philosopher's stone. And as it is part of man's ungodliness to believe his fellow-sinner more than his Creator, the Most High provided an unimpeachable testimony. He raised up Solomon. He made him healthy and handsome—wise and brilliant. He poured wealth into his lap, till it ran over; he made him absolute monarch of the finest kingdom which the world at that time offered; and, instead of savages and pagans, gave him for his subjects a civilized and a religious people. And that he might not be distracted by wars and rumors of wars, he put into his hand a peaceful sceptre, and saved him from the hardships of the field and the perils of the fight. And thus endowed and thus favored, Solomon commenced the search after happiness. Everything except godly, he devoted himself to the art of enjoyment. And in carrying on his own experiment he unwittingly, but effectually, became God's demonstration. Into the crucible he cast rank and beauty, wealth and learning; and, as a flux, he added youth and genius; and then, with all the ardor of his vehement nature, he urged the furnace to its whitest glow. But when the grand projection took place, from all the costly ingredients the entire residuum was, Vanity of vanities! And ere he left the laboratory, he made ink of the ashes; and in the confessions of a converted worldling, he was constrained to write one of the saddest books in all the Bible.

His first recourse was knowledge. Communing with his own heart, he said, "Lo, I am come to great estate, and have gotten more wisdom than all they that have been before me in Jerusalem: yea, my heart had great experience of wisdom and knowledge. And I gave my heart to know (more) wisdom, and to know madness and folly (that is, mirth and satire): I perceived that this also is vexation of spirit. For in much wisdom is much grief: and he that increaseth knowledge increaseth sorrow." And, as he adds elsewhere, "Of making many books there is no end; and much study is a weariness to the flesh."

No, no. *Carpe horam.* Life is short, and learning slow. Quit that dingy study, and out into the laughing world. Make a bonfire of these books, and fill your reed-quiver with bird-bolts. Exchange the man of letters for the man of pleasure. And so he did. "I gave myself to wine, I made me great works, I builded me houses, I planted me vineyards." But here, too, he was destined to disappointment. For the coarse pleasures of the carouse and the wine-cup his cultivated mind had little affinity; and when next morning revealed the faded chaplets, the goblets capsized, and the red wine-pools on the floor of the banquet-hall; when the merry-making of yesternight only lived in the misery of the morning, he exclaimed, "Such laughter is mad; and such mirth, what doeth it?" And so of the more elegant pastimes—the palace, the fish-pond, the flower-garden, the menagerie,—the enjoyment ended when the plan was executed; and as soon as the collection was completed, the pleasure of the collector ceased. "Then I looked on all the works that my hands had wrought, and on the labor that I had labored to do: and, behold, all was vanity and vexation of spirit, and there was no profit under the sun."

But there still remained one solace. There must be something very sweet in absolute power. Though the battle has been going on for six thousand years, and the odds are overwhelming—a million resisting one—yet still the love of power is so tremendous,—to say to one, Go, and he goeth; and to another, Do this, and he doeth it—the right to say this is so delicious, that sooner or later, the million lose the battle, and find the one their master. Now, this ascendency over others Solomon possessed to a rare degree. "The Preacher was king in Jerusalem." He was absolute monarch there. And to flatter his instinct of government still more, surrounding states and sovereigns all did homage at Jerusalem. But no sooner did he find his power thus supreme and unchallenged, than he began to be visited with misgivings as to his successor—misgivings for which the sequel showed that there was too good reason. "Yea, I hated all the labor which I had taken under the sun, because I should leave it unto the man that shall be after me. And who knoweth whether he shall be a wise man or a fool? Yet shall he have rule over all my labor wherein I have labored, and wherein I have showed myself wise under the sun. This is also vanity."

And I need not say how the experience of most worldlings has been Solomon's sorrow repeated, with the variations incident to altered circumstances, and the diminished intensity to be expected in feebler men—vanity and vexation of spirit all over again. And as we are sometimes more impressed by modern instances than by Bible examples, we could call into court nearly as many witnesses as there have been hunters of happiness—mighty Nimrods in the chase of Pleasure, and Fame, and Power. We might ask the statesman, and, as we wished him a happy new year, Lord Dundas would answer, "It had need to be happier than the last, for I never knew one happy day in it." We might ask the successful lawyer, and the wariest, luckiest, most self-complacent of them all would answer, as Lord

Eldon was privately recording when the whole Bar envied the Chancellor,—"A few weeks will send me to dear Encombe, as a short resting-place between vexation and the grave." We might ask the golden millionaire, "You must be a happy man, Mr. Rothschild." "Happy!—me happy! What! happy, when just as you are going to dine you have a letter placed in your hand, saying, 'If you do not send me £500, I will blow your brains out?"' Happy! when you have to sleep with pistols at your pillow? We might ask the clever artist, and our gifted countryman would answer of whose latter days a brother writes, "In the studio, all the pictures seemed to stand up like enemies to receive me. This joy in labor, this desire for fame, what have they done for him? The walls of this gaunt sounding place, the frames, even some of the canvasses, are furred with damp. In the little library, where he painted last, was the word 'Nepenthe?' written interrogatingly with white chalk on the wall."* We might ask the world-famed

* Memoir of David Scott, R.S.A.

warrior, and get for another answer the "Miserere" of the Emperor-monk,* or the sigh of a broken heart from St. Helena. We might ask the brilliant courtier, and Lord Chesterfield would tell us, "I have enjoyed all the pleasures of the world, and I do not regret their loss. I have been behind the scenes. I have seen all the coarse pulleys and dirty ropes which move the gaudy machines; and I have seen and smelt the tallow candles which illuminate the whole decorations, to the astonishment of an ignorant audience." We might ask the dazzling wit, and, faint with a glut of glory, yet disgusted with the creatures who adored him, Voltaire would condense the essence of his existence into one word, "*Ennui.*" And we might ask the world's poet, and we would be answered with an imprecation by that splendid genius,† who

"Drank every cup of joy, heard every trump
Of fame; drank early, deeply drank; drank draughts
That common millions might have quenched—then died
Of thirst, because there was no more to drink."

* Charles V.

† Byron.

But without going so far as these historic instances, I make my appeal to all the candor and self-knowledge here present, and I ask, Who is there that, apart from God's favor, has ever tasted solid joy and satisfaction of spirit? You have perhaps tried learning. You have wearied your flesh acquiring some branch of knowledge, or mastering the arcana of some science; and you promised yourself that, when once you were an adept, it would introduce you to a circle of transcendental friends, or would drown you in a flood of golden fame. You won the friends, and, apart from this special accomplishment, you found them so full of petty feuds and jealousies, so cold-hearted or so coarse-minded, that you inwardly abjured them, and vowed that you must follow learning for its own rewards; or you won the fame—you secured the prize—you caught the coveted distinction, and like the senior wrangler,* you found that you had "grasped a shadow." Or you tried some course of gaiety. You said, "Go to now—I

* Henry Martyn.

will prove thee with mirth; therefore enjoy pleasure." You dressed—you took pains with your appearance; you studied the art of pleasing. But even self-love could not disguise that some rival was more dazzling, more graceful and self-possessed, and had made a more brilliant impression: and you came home mortified at your own sheepishness and rustic blundering; or, if content to mingle passively in others' merriment, tattling with the talkers, and drifting along the tide of drollery, was there no pensive reflection as, late at night, you sought your dwelling?—did you not say of laughter, "It is mad? and of mirth, What doeth it?" Or, perhaps, at some pleasant time of the year, you made up a famous ploy. And the excursion went off, but the promised enjoyment never came up. Mountain breezes did not blow away your vexing memories, nor did the soft sea-wind heal your wounded spirit. In the rapid train you darted swiftly, but at the journey's end you were mortified to find that your evil temper had travelled by the same conveyance. And though it was a classic or a sacred stream into which you looked, not even Arethusa nor Siloah could polish from off your countenance the furrows of carking anxiety, or the frown of crossness which wrinkled there. The truth is, all will be vanity to the heart which is vile, and all will be vexation to the spirit which the peace of God is not possessing. When you remember how vast is the soul of man, and also what a mighty virus of depravity pervades it, you might as well ask, How many showers will it need to make the salt ocean fresh? as ask, How many mercies will it need to make a murmuring spirit thankful and happy? You might as soon ask, How many buckets of water must you pour down the crater of Etna before you convert the volcano into a cool and crystal *jet-d'eau?* as ask, How many bounties must Providence pour into a worldling's spirit before it that spirit will cease to evaporate them into vanity, or send them fuming back in complaint and vexation?—

> "Attempt how vain—
> With things of earthly sort, with aught but God,

With aught but moral excellence, truth, and love—
To satisfy and fill the immortal soul!
To satisfy the ocean with a drop;
To marry immortality to death;
And with the unsubstantial shade of time,
To fill the embrace of all eternity!"*

* Pollok's "Course of Time" book iv.

LECTURE III.

A Greater than Solomon.

"The Queen of the South . . . . came from the uttermost parts of the earth to hear the wisdom of Solomon; and, behold, a greater than Solomon is here."—MATT. xii. 42.

IT was autumn with the Hebrew commonwealth. Like withered leaves from the sapless tree, the Jews easily parted from the parent Palestine, and were blown about, adventurers in every land; and like that fungous vegetation which rushes up when nobler plants have faded, formalism and infidelity were rankly springing everywhere; and it was only a berry on the topmost bough—some mellow Simeon or Zacharias—that reminded you of the rich old piety. The sceptre had not quite departed from Judah, but he who held it was a puppet in the Gentiles' hand; and with ship-less harbors, and silent oracles, with Roman sentinels on every public building, and Roman tax-gatherers in every town, patriotism felt too surely, that from the land of Joshua and Samuel, of Elijah and Isaiah, of David and Solomon, the glory was at last departing. The sky was lead, the air a winding-sheet; and every token told that a long winter was setting in. It was even then, amid the short days and sombre sunsets of the waning dynasty, when music filled the firmament, and in the city of David a mighty Prince was born. He grew in stature, and in due time was manifested to Israel. And what was the appearance of this greater than Solomon? What were his royal robes? The attire of a common Nazarene. What were his palaces? A carpenter's cottage, which He sometimes exchanged for a fisherman's hut. Who were his Ministers and his Court attendants? Twelve peasants. And what was his state chariot? None could He afford; but in one special procession He rode on a borrowed ass. Ah! said we so? His royal robe was heaven's splendor, whenever

He chose to let it through; and Solomon, in all his glory, was never arrayed like Jesus on Tabor. His palace was the heaven of heavens; and when a voluntary exile from it, little did it matter whether his occasional lodging were a rustic hovel, or Herod's halls. If fishermen were his friends, angels were his servants; and if the borrowed colt was his triumphal charger, the sea was proud when, from crest to crest of its foaming billows, it felt his majestic footsteps moving; and when the time had arrived for returning to his Father and his God, the clouds lent the chariot, and obsequious airs upbore Him in their reverent hands. Solomon's pulpit was a throne, and he had an audience of kings and queens. The Saviour's synagogue was a mountain-side—his pulpit was a grassy knoll or a fishing-boat—his audience were the boors of Galilee; and yet, in point of intrinsic greatness, Solomon did not more excel the children playing in the market-place, than He who preached the Sermon on the Mount excelled King Solomon.

Looking at Solomon as a Teacher, the first

thing that strikes us is, that he was a great querist. Next to the man who can answer a question thoroughly, is the man who can ask it clearly. Our world is full of obscure misery —dark wants and dim desiderata: like a man in a low fever, its whole head is sick, and its whole heart faint; but it can neither fix exactly on the focus of disease, nor give an intelligent account of its sensations. But in this respect Solomon was the mouth-piece of humanity. Speaking for himself, he has so described the symptoms, that a whole ward—an entire world of fellow-sufferers—may take him for their spokesman. "These are exactly my feelings. I have experienced all that he describes. I am just such another fitful anomaly —just such a constant self-contradiction. One day I wish time to fly faster; another I am appalled to find that so little remains. One day I believe that I shall die like the brutes; and, frantic in thinking that a spirit so capacious is to perish so soon, I chafe around my cage, and beat those bars of flesh which inclose a captive so god-like; I try to burst that cell which is ere long to be a sepulchre: anon I am content, and I say, 'Eat, drink, and be merry, for to-morrow you die:' and no sooner is the carnival over than I start up, conscious of my crime—descrying the forgotten judgment-seat, and aghast at my own impiety in embruting an heir of immortality. One day I deny myself, and save up a fortune for my son and successor; another, it strikes me he may prove a prodigal, and I fling the hoard away. Now it seizes me that I must needs be famous; and then I grow disgusted with the praise of fools. What will cure a broken heart? What will fill an abysmal gulf? What will make a crooked nature upright? What will restore his Creator unto man, and man unto himself?"

And Jesus answers: "Believe in God and believe in me, and that faith will heal heart-trouble. Hunger after righteousness, and your craving spirit will be filled. The words that I speak unto you are spirit and life: imbibe them, ponder them, delight in them, and they will satisfy the vastest desires of the most eager soul. What will make the crooked upright?

Be born again. What will restore the Creator to revolted man? God so loved the world, that he gave his only-begotten Son, that whosoever believeth in him should have eternal life." And thus, one by one, the great Evangelist answers the queries of the great Ecclesiastes. And if the sage has done a service, who, in articulate words, describes the symptoms of the great disease, how incomparably greater is the service done by the Saviour, who prescribes the remedy! After all, Solomon is only an eloquent patient; Jesus is the Divine Physician.

Again: Solomon's teaching is mainly negative. Five centuries later, it was the business of the wisest Greek to teach his brethren knowledge of their ignorance. And so dexterously did he manage his oblique mirrors—so many of his countrymen did he surprise with side-views and back-views of themselves; so much fancied knowledge did he confute, and so many Athenians did he put out of conceit with themselves, that at last the Athenians lost conceit of him, and killed the mortifying missionary. And, like Socrates, Solomon is an apostle of sincerity. His pen is the point of a diamond; and as it touches many of this world's boasted jewels, it shows that they are only colored crystal. His sceptre is a rod of iron, and as it enabled him to command all pleasures, so it enables him to prove their nullity; and before his indignant stroke they crash like potsherds, and dissipate in dust. But more sincere than Socrates. His tests, his probes, his solar lamp, the Greek employed for his neighbors' benefit; such an awful earnestness had God's Spirit enkindled in the Hebrew sage, that his grand struggle was against self-deception: and the illusions on which he spends his hottest fury are the phantoms which have befooled himself. Socrates gossips; Solomon communes with his own heart. Socrates gets his comrade to confess; Solomon makes his own confession. And so terrible is his intensity, that if it be well for our modern idoloclasts and showers-up of shams that there is no Socrates now-a-days to show them to themselves, it will be well for us all if we take a pattern from Solomon's noble fidelity, and if we strive after his stern self-knowledge. And yet the result was mainly negative. He had dived deep enough into his nature to find that there was no genuine goodness there; and from the height of his stately intellect he swept a wide horizon, and reported that within his field of view there was perceptible no genuine happiness. If he was taller than other men, he was sorry to announce that, far as he could see, no fountain of joy now sprang in this desert: no tree of life grew here-away. If he was stronger than other men, he had bad news for them: he had tried the gate of Eden, and shoved it and shaken it: but he feared no mortal shoulders could move it on its hinges, nor any human contrivance force it from its fastenings.

But if Solomon in his teaching was mainly negative, Jesus was as mainly positive. Solomon shook his head, and told what happiness is not: Jesus opened his lips, and enunciated what it is. Solomon said, "Knowledge is vanity. Power is vanity. Mirth is vanity.

Man and all man's pursuits are perfect vanity." Jesus said, "Humility is blessedness. Meekness is blessedness. Purity of heart is blessedness. God is blessed for evermore, and most blessed is the creature that is likest God. Holiness is happiness." "We labor and find no rest," said Solomon. Jesus answered, "Come unto me, all ye that labor, and I will give you rest." "All is vanity," sighed the Preacher. "In the world ye shall have tribulation, but in me ye shall have peace," replied the Saviour. "What is truth?" asks Ecclesiastes. "I am the truth," returns the Divine Evangelist. Solomon was tall enough to scan the most of earth and see an expanse of sorrow; the Son of Man knew all that is in heaven, and could tell of a Comforter who fills with peace unspeakable the soul immersed in outward misery. Solomon could tell that the gate of bliss is closed against human effort. Jesus has the key of David, and opens what Adam shut; and into the Father's propitious presence He undertakes to usher all who come through Him. Solomon composed Earth's epitaph, and on the tomb of the species wrote, All is Vanity. Accustomed to date men's history from their death, Jesus substituted, All is Heaven or Hell.*

Nay, so positive was the Saviour's teaching, that, in order to understand him rightly, we must remember that he was not only the Prophet, but the doctrine; not only the Oracle uttering God's truth, but his very self that Truth. Other prophets could tell what God's mind is: Jesus was that mind. "The law"—a portion of God's will—"was given by Moses; but grace and truth"—the gracious reality, the truthful plenitude of the Divine perfections, "came by Jesus Christ." He was the express image of the Father. He was the Word Incarnate. And to many a query of man's wistful spirit, He was the embodied answer. Is there any immortality to this soul? Is there any second life to this body? "In my Father's house are many mansions. I go to prepare a place for you, and I will come again and re-

* Matt. v. 3–12; xi. 28–30. John xvi. 33; xiv. 6, 16, 17. Rev. iii. 7. John x. 9; vi. 37. Luke xvi. 19–31.

ceive you to myself." "I am the Resurrection and the Life: he that believeth in me shall never die: I will raise him up at the last day." Is there any mediation betwixt man and his Maker?—is there any forgiveness of sin? "I am the way. Whatsoever ye shall ask the Father in my name, He will give it you. Go in peace: thy sins are forgiven thee." Is there any model of excellence exempt from all infirmity?—any pattern in which the Most High has perfect complacency? "He was holy and harmless, separate from sinners." "This is my beloved Son, in whom I am well pleased: hear ye Him." Solomon was wise; but Jesus was Wisdom. Solomon had more understanding than all the ancients; but Jesus was that eternal Wisdom of which Solomon's genius was a borrowed spark—of which the deep flood of Solomon's information was only an emitted rill.

To which we only add the contrast in their tone. Each had a certain grandeur. Solomon's speech was regal. It had both the imperial amplitude and the autocratic emphasis,

—stately, decisive, peremptory. But the Saviour's was Divine. There was no pomp of diction, but there was a God-like depth of meaning; and such was its spontaneous majesty, that the hearer felt, How easily He could speak a miracle! And miracles He often spake; but so naturally did they emerge from his discourse, and so noiselessly did they again subside into its current, that we as frequently read of men astonished at his doctrine, as of men amazed at his doings. But though both spake with authority—the one with authority as a king of men, the other with authority as the Son of God—there is a wonderful difference in point of the pervasive feeling. Like a Prometheus chained to the rock of his own remorse, the Preacher pours forth his mighty woes in solitude, and, truly human, is mainly piteous of itself. Consequently his enthroned misery—his self-absorbed and stately sorrow, moves you to wonder, rather than to weep; and, as when you look at a gladiator dying in marble, in your compassion there is not much of tenderness. But though greater in his sorrows, the Saviour was also greater in his sympathies; and though silent about his personal anguish, there is that in his mild aspect which tells each who meets it, If his grief be great, his love is greater. And whilst Solomon is so king-like that he does not ask you to be his friend, the Saviour is so God-like that he solicits your affection, and so brotherly that he wins it. Indeed, here is the mystery of godliness—God manifest in flesh, that flesh may see how God is love; and that through the loveliness of Jesus we may be attracted and entranced into the love of God. O melancholy monarch! how funereal is thy tread, as thou pacest up and down thy echoing galleries, and disappearest in the valley of Death-shadow, ever sounding—Vanity of vanities! O Teacher blessed! how beautiful are thy feet on the mountains, publishing peace! How benign thy outstretched hand, which, to the sinner weeping over it, proves God's golden sceptre of forgiveness, and which then clasps that sinner's hand and guides him to glory! O Thou greater than Solomon! "let me see thy countenance, let me hear thy voice; for sweet is thy voice, and thy countenance is comely."

A greater than Solomon. The cedar palace has long since yielded to the torch of the spoiler; but the home which Jesus has prepared for his disciples is a house not made with hands, eternal in the heavens. Thorns and thistles choke the garden of Engedi, and the moon is no longer mirrored in the fish-ponds of Heshbon; but no brier grows in the paradise above, and nothing will ever choke or narrow that fountain whence life leaps in fulness, or stagnate that still expanse where the Good Shepherd leads his flock at glory's noon. And Solomon—the wonder of the world—his grave is with us at this day; his flesh has seen corruption; and he, too, must hear the voice of the Son of Man, and come forth to the great account: but Jesus saw no corruption. Him hath God raised up, and made a Prince and a Saviour; and hath given him authority to execute judgment, because He is the Son of Man. And, reverting to the allusion of our outset: Solomon effloresced from his country's golden age; a greater than Solomon appeared when miry clay was mixing with its age of iron. Solomon was, so to speak, an effusion of his age, as well as its brightest ornament: the Son of Mary was an advent and an alien—a star come down to sojourn in a cavern—a root of Deity from our earth's dry ground. But though it was the Hebrew winter when he came, he did not fail nor wax discouraged. He taught, he lived, he fulfilled all righteousness—he loved, he died. It was winter wheat: but the corn fell into the ground ungrudgingly; for as he sowed his seeds of truth, the Saviour knew that he was sowing the summer of our world. And, as, one by one, these seeds spring up, they fetch with them a glow more genial; for every saved soul is not only something for God's garner; but an influence for mankind. Already of that handful of corn which this greater Solomon scattered on the mountain-tops of Galilee, the first-fruits are springing; and by-and-by the fruit shall shake like Lebanon, and the Church's citizens shall be abundant as grass of the earth. On the wings of prophecy it is hastening towards us; and every prayer and every mission speeds it on—our world's latter summer-burst, our earth's perennial June—when the name of Jesus shall endure forever, and be continued as long as the sun: when men shall be blessed in Him, and all nations shall call him blessed.

So great is this Prince of prophets, that the least in his kingdom is greater than Solomon. The saint is greater than the sage, and discipleship to Jesus is the pinnacle of human dignity. In Him are hid all the treasures of wisdom, and all the germs of undeveloped goodness. He is the true theology, the perfect ethics, the supreme philosophy; and no words can limit the mental ascendency and moral beauty to which that young man may aspire, who, in all the susceptibility of an adoring affection, consecrates himself to the service and society of the Son of God. My brothers! is it a presumptuous hope that, even whilst I speak, some of you feel stirring within you the desire to join yourselves to blessedness by joining yourselves to Jesus? Is it too much to hope that some of you, who are Christian young men already, are wishing and praying that God would make your characters less commonplace, and render your influences in your day more abundant and benign? Is it too much to hope that, even from this rapid survey, some shall retire with a happy consciousness,—Blessed be God! I belong to a kingdom which cannot be moved, and am embarked in a cause which cannot be defeated? Is it too much to hope that some one who has found, in regard to godless enjoyment, "All is vanity," may now be led to exclaim, with the gifted youth to whom our poet-laureate has inscribed "In Memoriam," "Lord, I have viewed this world over, in which thou hast set me; I have tried how this and that thing will fit my spirit, and the design of my creation, and can find nothing on which to rest, for nothing here doth itself rest; but such things as please me for a while in some degree, vanish and flee as shadows from before me. Lo! I come to thee—the Eternal Being—the Spring of Life—the Centre of Rest—the Stay of the Creation—the Fulness of all things. I join myself to Thee; with Thee I will lead my life and spend my days, with whom I am to dwell forever, expecting, when my little time is over, to be taken up into thine own eternity."*

* From a deeply interesting account of Arthur H. Hallam, in the "North British Review," for February, 1851.

LECTURE IV.

The Vestibule of Vanity.

READ ECCLES. I. 2–11.

"Vanity of vanities, saith the Preacher, vanity of vanities· all is vanity."

ECCLESIASTES is Solomon the Prodigal, re-exhibited by Solomon the Preacher. The wisest of worldlings here opens a window in his bosom and shows us all those fluctuating emotions and conflicting passions which whirl and eddy in every heart whose currents run opposite ways.

In this separate enclosure, so unlike the surrounding Scripture; such a contrast to the joyous parterre which blossoms beside it,* the traveller has planted the wormwood and the rue, all the bitter herbs and the lurid which he

* The Song of Solomon.

gathered in his grand tour of vanity; and he has left them, at once, a memorial and a medicine—a record of his own painful experiences, and a corrective to curious speculation and sensual indulgence.

The right way to understand Ecclesiastes is to read it alongside of the other Scriptures. Obscure in itself we must take the daylight at the end as a lamp, to guide us as we go; and, for its duskier recesses, we may borrow the bright lantern of prophets and evangelists. We shall thus not only find its perusal safe and profitable, but, as its dark sayings flash into significance, and its negations are filled up by counterpart verities, in its very sternness we shall recognize another feature of Revelation's symmetry. Solomon will tell us the vanity of doubt; the rest of the Bible will tell us the blessedness of a firm belief. Solomon will tell us the misery of the selfist, who seeks to be his own all in all; the evangelists will tell us the blessedness of a true benevolence. Solomon will tell us the vanity of the creature; the rest of the Bible reveals the sufficiency of the great Creator. Solomon will tell us how he amassed unprecedented riches, but found no comfort in them: his shepherd sire will answer by anticipation, "My cup runneth over. Surely goodness and mercy shall follow me all the days of my life; and I shall dwell in the house of the Lord forever." Solomon will tell us how, in a palace and a crown, and in imperial fame, he found nothing but chagrin: Jesus will answer, "In the world ye shall have tribulation; but in me ye shall have peace." Solomon the sage will tell us, "Vanity of vanities; all is vanity." Solomon the saint will answer, "O Saviour, thy love is better than wine. Draw me, and I will run after thee. Tarry with me until the day break and the shadows flee away."

This passage is the preamble to the book. And it is an appropriate preface. Like sentinels of cypress, cold and glaucous, at a winter-garden's gate, like sphinxes of solemn stone flanking the entrance of the Silent Land, this prologue is a fit introduction to the mournful story we are about to read, and ushers us at once into its realms of dreariness.

As much as if he said, "It is all a weary go-round. This system of things is a perpetual self-repetition,—quite sickening. One generation goes, another comes. The sun rises, and the sun goes down. That was what the sun did yesterday, and what I expect it will do to-morrow. The wind blows north, and the wind blows south; and this is all it has been doing for these thousand years. The rivers run into the sea, and it would be some relief to find that sea up-filling; to perceive the clear waters wetting the dry shingle, and brimming up to the green fields, and floating the boats and fishes up into the forest: but even that inconvenient novelty is denied us; for though the Nile and many a river have been tumbling a world of water into it, this tide will not overstep its margin; the flood still bulges, but still refuses to cross its bounds. Words* themselves are weariness, and it would tire you to enumerate those everlasting mutations and

* דברים, so rendered by Knobel and others.

busy uniformities which make up this endless screw of existence. There are no novelties, no wonders, no discoveries. This universe does not yield an eye-full, an ear-full, to its occupant. The present only repeats the past, the future will repeat them both. The inventions of to-day are the forgotten arts of yesterday, and our children will forget our wisdom, only to have the pleasure of fishing up, as new prodigies, our obsolete truisms. There is no new thing under the sun, yet no repose. Perpetual functions and transient objects,—permanent combinations, yet shifting atoms, sameness, yet incessant change, make up the monotonous medley. Woe's me for this weary world!"

In such feelings I think it possible that a few of my hearers may sympathize. To you it is very painful—this fugacity of time—this flight of years and ages—this coming and going of the generations. And to you it is very oppressive—this monotony of life—this constant recurrence of the same small pleasures—and this total absence of any magnificent enjoyment. You both want something of which you may say, "See, this is new," and something of which you may feel, "Now this is good—this is noble: here is something which will never pass away: a joy that will be my comrade through eternity—for neither it nor I shall ever die." From such vexing thoughts might you not escape by taking refuge in one permanence and one variety to which the royal Preacher does not here advert? I mean the soul's immortality, and the renewed soul's perpetual juvenescence; that attribute of mind which makes it the survivor of all changes, and that faculty of regenerate humanity which renders old things new, and suffuses with perpetual freshness things the most familiar.

It is true that, compared with many visible objects, man is ephemeral. Compared with the sun that shines over him—the air which fans him—the ocean on which he floats, his "duration is a swift decay." And there is much pensiveness in the thought of his own frailty. To look out, as we were last week looking, on the plenitude of summer,—to view the exuberance of verdure in the woods, and the soft warmth upon the waters—to inhale the fragrance of roses, mingling with earth's ripeness, and think how soon our eyes must shut forever on that landscape—how soon aromatic breezes and blushing flowers shall stir no animation in our tombs,—to think that there will be as much of ecstasy in the season, but in that ecstasy we shall be no sharers; or, as the poet has expressed it in his "Farewell to the Brook,"—

> Flow down, cold rivulet, to the sea,
> Thy tribute wave deliver;
> No more by thee, my steps shall be,
> Forever, and forever.
>
> But here will sigh thine alder-tree,
> And here thine aspen shiver;
> And here by thee, will hum the bee,
> Forever, and forever.
>
> A thousand suns will stream on thee,
> A thousand moons will quiver;
> But not by thee, my steps shall be,
> Forever, and forever.*

In such contemplations there is a deep pathos, and to surrender the spirit to their habitual

* Tennyson.

mastery would be to live a life of constant melancholy.

But, whatever may be the sensations of worldlings, these ought not to be the feelings of Christians. Jesus Christ hath brought immortality to light through the Gospel. He has taught us that amidst all sublunary perpetuities, the most perpetual is the soul of man. He has assured us that the man who believes in Himself shall never die, and that of all things which ever tenanted this planet, the most enduring are Himself and those whom faith and affection make one with Himself: the great Alpha and Omega, and all the redeemed existence included in his own.

But more than that, have you thought, my friends, on the immortalizing faculty of your own immortal minds? The soul of man is not only earth's true amaranth, but earth's only antiseptic. It is only in that soul that this visible creation will by-and-by exist at all. It is only in your deathless memory that its fair scenes and curious objects will, ere long, survive; but there they can never die. Already the face of things has entirely changed since the days of Solomon. No limner has preserved the aspect of Palestine as his poetic father viewed it. But there are memories in which it lives. The well of Bethlehem—its streets, its houses, and its stables, as they stood a thousand years before the Saviour of the world was born in one of them; the copse where the young shepherd cut his crook, and the bazaar where he bought his harp; the slopes tufted with hyssop and elastic with thyme, where his broad-tailed flocks cropped the herbage, and the trees where they rested at noon; the muster of the Philistines on one side of the torrent, and Israel's tents on the other—all these have vanished from under the sun, but all these are still vivid in the spectator's strengthened memory. And there, too, are still depicted portraits which the artists of earth can only imagine;—Jesse's manly port as, with yeoman pride, he stalked out and in among his thriving herds and soldier sons,—Samuel's reverend visage as he poured the anointing oil,—Goliath's mighty bulk as he fell over on the quaking turf,—Jonathan's tearful smile as he bade farewell for that fatal Gilboa. And even so, if you be the children of God, this earth is your unfading heritage. Its best things will subsist as long as you care to preserve them. And, even after that earth and all its works, all its present features and all its present productions have disappeared, there will be as many records of creation as there are holy recollections in heaven. When the aspen and the alder, when the bee in the fox-glove, and the roses round the bower, are extinct species, or are only enshrined in the amber of celestial reminiscence; you will still remember what like earth's sanctuaries looked, and how its summers shone. Or should even sun and moon grow pale, their image will endure so long as you remember the happy hour when you gave yourself to God: so long as you remember the mossy bank where first, in the Saviour's invitations, you read your title to a mansion in the skies: so long as you remember the bright winter-night returning from the country communion, when the peace of God was a full tide in your bosom, and in the melting admiration of redeeming love, you looked up into the heavens and said, "What is man, that thou art mindful of him?" Ah! yes; the immortality of material forms is the immortality of the soul of man.

And of these material forms it is the highest function,—so to speak, it is their greatest privilege, to tell on man's immortality;—to get so blended with man's being as to survive the wreck of matter, and share that existence which alone is undissolving. And though this suggests some painful thoughts, though it is sad to think how objects of cupidity and avarice, and how the incentives to unholy passion may survive only in that self-accusing conscience which they helped to make a child of hell, boasting no monument beyond such miscreant memory: still there is a fitness, and one feels happy in the thought that God's good works shall be eternally embalmed in those immortal natures which they have helped to make good and beautiful, and shall never die so long as those spirits live to whose growth in grace they once gave aliment. Generations will cease to come and go. The earth in its present arrangements, will not "abide forever." It will soon be burned up, along with all its works. Its present races will be annihilated, or only recognized as dim fossils in the calcined strata; and the very books which have been engraven and painted to represent their forms, shall perish in the mighty conflagration. But even then there will be tablets of Nature numerous as the spirits of the just made perfect; and what museums have failed to keep will be still secure in the fire-proof cabinets of saintly recollection. No eagle will then poise in the vacant firmament, but its restful gyrations, its sunward aspiring, will still be present to that mind which used to associate with it the self-renovating efforts of prayer: "They that wait upon the Lord shall renew their strength: they shall mount up on wings as eagles." And from another planet the pilgrim coming would vainly search for Syria's far-famed lily: but its image still wlil linger both in the memory and the character of that modest disciple to whom Jesus said not in vain, "Consider the lilies, and be clothed like them." There will then be no Jacob's well; but its deep shaft and shady canopy will still be pictured in her memory, who, one summer afternoon, found resting there a stranger, and obtained from him water of everlasting life. And there will be no Patmos then, but its creeks and caverns will all be mapped in his affectionate fancy, who found it the open gate of the New Jerusalem; and who will recall the lizards on its cliffs and the little fishes in its pools, with Apocalyptic light and Sabbath joy around them.

There is another sense in which these material agencies are working a moral progress, and so promoting the scheme of God. Looking up at the weather-cock, says the sage of vanity, "Woe's me for this weary wind! There, it was south this morning, and now it is north! How many ways it blows, and never long the same! What's the use of all this whirling? And if it were only to make the vane spin round, the air as well might stagnate: there were no need of such wasted power. But whilst the valetudinarian is looking at the vane, the wind is careering over a continent, and doing the Creator's work in a hundred lands. It has called at yon city, fetid with miasma and groaning with pestilence; and, with its besom of brisk pinions, it has swept the plague away. It has looked into yon haven, and found a forest of laden ships sleeping over their freights, and it has chased them all to sea. And finding the harvest arrested in a broad and fertile realm—the earth chapped, and the crops withering,—it is now hurrying with that black armament of clouds to drench it in lifesome irrigation. To narrow observation or to selfishness that wind is an annoyance: to faith it is God's angel,* forwarding the mighty plan. 'Tis a boisterous night, and Pictish savages curse the noisy blast which shakes their peat-hovels round their ears; but that noisy blast has landed the Gospel on St. Andrew's shore. It blows a fearful tempest, and it sets some rheumatic joints on

* Ps. civ. 3, 4.

aching; but the morrow shows dashed in pieces the awful Armada which was fetching the Spanish Inquisition to our British Isle. The wind blows east, and detains James's ships at Harwich; but it guides King William to Torbay. Yes, "the wind blows south and the wind blows north; it whirleth about continually, and returneth again according to its circuits." But in the course of these circuits the wind has blown to our little speck of sea-girt Happiness, the Gospel, and Protestantism, and civil and religious liberty. And so, not of our islet only, but of our globe entire, and its continuous population. So far as the individual is concerned, so far as it affects the weather-index in the wind, there may be little seeming progress; nay, so far as it concerns any plan which society proposes to itself, the favoring gale may shift and shift again, and the story of a nation be little better than the register of a stationary vane pirouetting on its windy pivot; but so far as affects the scheme of God, there is an *aura* in the universe which always drives one way. Predestination is a vane which never vibrates, and Providence a wind which never whirls about. The breath of God's Spirit and the strength of God's purpose are steadily wafting our world and all the worlds in one mighty convoy towards God's appointed haven in the distant future. So cheer up, Solomon, and all ye sighing sages; cheer up, you that complain of the sameness and insipidity of mundane affairs. Cheer up, you that pine for some grand disclosure, and long for something that will fill your eye and satisfy your ear. When in the harbor of God's finished mystery, the sails of history are furled, and the eternal anchor is dropped—when the last generation falls in and the last holy intelligence comes home, you who have so often asked, Is there anything whereof it may be said, See, this is new? you will see "all things made new;" you, whose eye has never been satisfied with seeing, will be satisfied when you see Him as He is; and you, whose ear was never satisfied with hearing, will long for nothing fuller when responsive to the overture which morning-stars sang so long ago, the grand *finale* shall burst from Infinitude exclaiming, "Blessing, and honor, and glory, and power, be unto Him that sitteth upon the throne, and to the Lamb, forever and ever."

If, as we have said, the immortality of material forms is only that which they achieve through the immortality of the human soul; and if the true glorification of matter is its sanctifying influence on regenerate mind, we may learn two lessons from our argument:

First, that there is no harm in a vivid susceptibility of those material appearances and influences with which God has replenished the universe. Some religionists would make contempt of the creation a test of piety; but they greatly err. It was of the material universe that six times over God said that it was "good." And it was in that material universe that the Son of God Incarnate evidently sought refreshment for his eyes when weary with viewing vanity. Yes, Jesus himself has taken to heaven some of its relics of Eden:

"Oh, Saviour, gone to God's right hand,
Yet the same Saviour still;
Graved on Thy heart is this lovely strand
And every fragrant hill."*

Secondly. But that susceptibility is good for nothing if it be not sanctified. There is an idolatry of nature. There are some whose God is the visible creation, and not the God and Father of our Lord Jesus Christ. And there is a voluptuousness in the enjoyment of nature. There are some to whom the landscape and its ingredients are neither the recreation fitting them for more active duties, nor the ladder of easy steps leading them up to adoring and loving thoughts of God; but, like the epicure over his viands, they sit down to the banquet as if they cared for no higher paradise. At this moment, when so many are panting for a purer air, and preparing to migrate to other scenes in search of it, it may be a word in season. Go, you that have worked hard for it—go and enjoy your holiday. But whithersoever you go, let all your religion go

* M'Cheyne's "Sea of Galilee."

with you. If you go among foreigners, instead of gruffness and *hauteur*, take with you Christian complaisance, and do justice at once to the good feeling of England and the courtesy of real religion. And whether among compatriots or foreigners, take with you the Sabbath-day. Keep its hours as sacred in the hired lodging or the inn, as you keep them in your own well-ordered home. Pray for the places where you sojourn, and as seeds for the eternal harvest, it were well if you could drop some good words or arresting tracts as you pass along. And then, when bursts of beauty or surprises of grandeur come in upon your soul, let the thought also come in of your "Father," who "made them all." And thus associated with the profitable books you read, or the Christian intercourse you enjoyed, or the efforts at usefulness you there put forth,—places which to the vacant mind recall no memories, and to the profligate are only identified with dissipation and riot,—will to you be fraught with pleasant recollections; and, thus beautified and sanctified, the resorts and recreations of earth will be worthy of a mental pilgrimage even from the bowers of Paradise Restored.

LECTURE V.

The Museum.

READ ECCLES. I. 12–18.

"In much wisdom is much grief; and he that increaseth knowledge increaseth sorrow."

SOLOMON'S first recourse was philosophy. He was a king, and he could pursue his researches on a splendid scale. We know that he collected natural curiosities from distant countries, and it is likely that he attracted to his court the learned of many lands. Nor is it improbable that he attained an insight to natural phenomena, possessed by none of his contemporaries. To the present day Eastern magicians invoke his name as if he were a controller of the elements; a circumstance from which some have very gratuitously inferred that he must have been a magician himself. But the fact is interesting. It looks as if tradition still preserved a recollection of certain prodigies which science enabled him to perform, and it would suggest that he was an experimenter as well as an observer.

But it was not only apes and peacocks, cedars and hyssop, which he studied, and the elements on which he experimented; he studied man. He looked at man's position in this world. He examined his story in time past. "He sought and searched out by wisdom concerning all things that are done under heaven;" "he saw all the works that are done under the sun." And he did not confine himself to grave generalities; he did not read solely the stately history of kings. "He gave his heart to know madness and folly," as well as "wisdom;" nor was he so pedantic as not to gather instruction from the frivolous and fantastic as well as from the august in human nature. His appetite for knowledge was omnivorous, and whilst hungering for the harvest he was thankful for crumbs.

The result was, satiety without satisfaction;

or rather, it was the sober certainty of "sorrow." "All the works done under the sun are vanity and vexation of spirit." Look at this Mesech of mortality! What a hot and noisy hive it is, and how each insect hums out and in on his consequential errands, till some night Death, the grim owner, comes and stifles all, and takes the honey. "I have seen all the works done under the sun;" I know their object, I know their result. It is comfort, soul-content for which the millions moil and bustle. For this the clodpole delves in the stiff clay, and the pearl-fisher dives in the deep lagoon. From his fragrant woods the herbalist of Gilead would fain distil it, and from his royal dainties the Asherite strives to confect it. With its rich cargoes the ships of Tarshish and the dromedaries of Midian have many a time been laden; but when the time came to open the bales, nothing was found save ocean-brine or desert sand. All was transmuted into vanity and vexation of spirit. "This sore travail hath God given to the sons of men." The very pursuit of knowledge is penal. The search after happiness is itself a sore punishment. Here, like a gin-horse, has the world been for ages tramping round and round, hoping to fetch up the golden bucket from the deep shaft of thought and effort; but alas! sin has cut the rope, and there is now no golden bucket at the end. Still, however, the blind gin-horse limps and wheezes on, and jades himself to death with this sore travail. I see the misery; I see not how to mend it. "That which is crooked cannot be made straight." There is a twist in man's destiny, a bias in man's will, a crook in man's constitution which science cannot rectify. "And that which is wanting cannot be numbered."

I have a list of those ingredients which constitute well-being, and which I am told that man once possessed, *e. g.*, peace of conscience, elasticity of temper, health, contentment, exemption from death, faith in the future; and I have made a survey of humanity and come back with an inventory of mere desiderata. These joys have vanished. The spoiler has been here. The regalia are rifled, and the onyx of Havilah has been torn from the crown which Adam wore in Paradise. And as the upshot of all I say, "Much wisdom is much grief, and he that increaseth knowledge increaseth sorrow." Happier that beggar child who can fancy his reed a sceptre, than that gray-haired monarch who knows that a sceptre is only gilded copper. Happier the fisher boy who, with his kettle, hopes to bail the sinking boat, than his wiser father who, through the widening leak, already sees their watery grave. Happier the peasant who fancies the magazine inexhaustible, than the governor who knows that it will be all consumed months before the harvest. In a world like this much science is much sorrow; for it is the knowledge of our penury,—the statistics of starvation,—the assurance that our case is desperate. Therefore, I break up my encyclopædic elysium, and on my temple of art inscribe, "Vanity and vexation of spirit:"—

> "Where ignorance is bliss;
> 'Tis folly to be wise."*

* As Lord Byron has expressed it, with his usual mixture

Unless it include the knowledge of the Living God, there is sorrow in much science; that is, the more a man knows, unless he also knows the Saviour, the sadder may we expect him to become. Of this we have an instance in a late philosopher, who, like Solomon, united to ardor of physical research a thoughtful and musing spirit, and who in his "Last Days of a Philosopher," has bequeathed to the world a manual of mournful "Consolations." It was not from any drawback in his outward lot, nor from any disappointment of his hopes, that Sir Humphrey Davy took leave of life so gloomily. Of the sons of science few have been so favored. In his grand discovery of the metallic bases, and in his more popular invention of the safety-lamp; in the command of a laboratory which opened a royal road to

of force and flippancy: "The lapse of ages *changes* all things: time, language, the earth, the bounds of the sea, the stars of the sky, and everything 'about, around, and underneath' man, *except man himself*, who has always been, and will always be an unlucky rascal. The infinite variety of lives conduct but to death, and the infinity of wishes lead but to disappointment. All the discoveries which have yet been made have multiplied little but existence."

chemistry, and in the splendid crowds who thronged to his lectures; from the moment that he found a generous patron till he became a Baronet of the United Kingdom, and President of the Royal Society, his whole career was a series of rare felicities. Nor was he the anchoret of science, a lonely and smoke-dried alchemist. He was a man of fashion, and, like Solomon, mingled "madness and folly" with graver pursuits. Yet with all his versatile powers,—orator, philosopher, poet; and with all his distinctions glittering around him, his heart still felt hollow, and in his later journals the expressive entry was, "Very miserable." What was it that he wanted? He himself has told us: "I envy no quality of mind or intellect in others,—not genius, power, wit, or fancy; but if I could choose what would be most delightful, and I believe most useful to me, I should prefer a firm religious belief to every other blessing; for it makes life a discipline of goodness, creates new hopes when all earthly hopes vanish, and throws over the decay, the destruction of existence, the most gorgeous of all lights, calling up the most delightful visions, where the sensualist and skeptic view only gloom, decay, and annihilation."

Whilst the philosopher has here truly said that nothing can fill the central gulf in man's spirit, except a sound religious belief, he speaks of its attainment despondingly; and probably he felt, what many have expressed, that it is not easy for a man of science to "receive the kingdom of God as a little child." It is possible that some one now present may be in the same predicament. You wish to believe, and are sorry to doubt; but you find that it is not easy to be at once the votary of science and the hearty disciple of Jesus Christ. When examining the evidence, or when reading the Bible itself, you are convinced that it is the Book of God. You recognize on its pages the same autograph with which you have long been familiar in the volume of creation, the same inimitable style of majesty, wisdom, goodness, and power; and you own that to refuse its authenticating credentials would be to set at defiance all the laws of evidence. You believe the Bible as long as you are in its own society; you love it as long as you commune with it. Looking into its face you perceive the halo, and tarrying in its precincts you are conscious of the Divinity indwelling. But passing away from it, and no longer warmed by its immediate inspiration; mingling with the cold materialisms which it is your province to explore; handling the dry preparations, or the gritty fossils, or the fuming retort,—the joy and the fragrance, and the vital influence of that Bible fade, and your devotion expires. Or, when you bore into the strata, and find yourself drilling down through cycles of unimagined time; or, when you look up into the starry vault, and find yourself transported into a measureless abyss, and its unnumbered worlds, —then all sorts of doubts and queries seem to rise like dragons from the deep, or they come trooping home like spectres from the dark immensity. You begin to feel yourself an atom in creation, and this world a mere mote in the universe, and you cannot help thinking revelation too great a boon for such an atom, and the Advent too great a wonder for such a world. You catch yourself saying, not in adoration, but in doubt, "What is man, that Thou art mindful of him? Or, what the son of man, that Thou shouldest visit him?"

Now I will not stop to suggest the cure for all these cavils. I might say that the best cure for nervous spectres or nightmare horrors, is to get a light, or look at something familiar and real; and the best cure for skeptic doubts is to look at the Bible itself. And I might farther say, that the mind is soundest and best constructed which receives all truth on its own evidence, and which does not suffer every wandering chimera to disturb a truth thus ascertained. But as it is a difficulty embarrassing to some thoughtful minds, we may just glance a little at the religious doubts occasioned by the extent of the universe.

Twenty years ago some English voyagers were standing on a flat beach within the Arctic Seas. From the excitement of their looks, the avidity with which they gazed into the ground, and the enthusiasm with which they looked around them, it was evident that they deemed it a spot of signal interest. But anything outwardly less interesting you could hardly imagine. On the one side, the coast retreated in low and wintry ridges, and on the other a pale ocean bore its icy freight beneath a watery sky, whilst under the travellers' feet lay neither bars of gold nor a gravel of gems. but blocks of unsightly limestone. Yet it was the centre of one of nature's greatest mysteries. It was the reward of years of adventure and hardship; it was the answer to the long aspirations and efforts of science; it was the Magnetic Pole. The travellers grudged that a place so important should appear so tame. They would have liked that it had been marked by some natural monument, a lofty peak or a singular rock. They were almost disappointed at not finding an iron needle as high as Cleopatra's own, or a loadstone as big as Mont Blanc.*

* "We could have wished that a place so important had possessed more of mark or note. I could even have pardoned any one among us who had been so romantic or absurd as to expect that the magnetic pole was an object as conspicuous

One day, a few summers since, sailing up the Rhine on a dull and windy afternoon, with little to look at but the sedgy banks and the storks exploring for reptiles among them—the vessel halted over against an old German town. We were looking languidly at its distant spires, and carelessly asked some one what town it was? "Worms." Worms! The battle-field of the Reformation; the little Armageddon where light and darkness, truth and error, liberty and despotism, the Son of God and the Prince of Darkness fought together not so long ago! Suddenly it seemed to swarm with Imperial troops and bluff old burghers; and had we been near enough we should have glanced up to the tiles on the house-tops, and in the streets looked out for Luther; but though it was the very spot where Protestantism gained its decisive victory, the spot where modern Europe threw off the cerements of the middle age, and emerged to life, to enterprise, and freedom, there was no outward sign to tell it,

and mysterious as the fabled mountain of Sindbad," &c.—*Ross's "Second Voyage."*

a dreary German town on a swampy plain—that was all.

Thus is it usually with memorable places. There is nothing external to arrest the eye; no gigantic landmark nor natural sign to serve for a *Siste, viator:* and the more refined and reflective do not grudge this. They feel that morally there is nothing so sublime as simplicity, and that it is God's way to work great wonders, not only by means of the things which are despised, but in despicable localities. Man is a materialist, and he tries to give a material magnitude to memorable places; but God chooses any common spot for the cradle of a mighty incident, or the home of a mighty spirit. Elbowing through Bread-street, amid trucks and drays and Cheapside tumult, who would fancy that here was the bower where the bard of Paradise was born; or looking up to that small window in the Canongate, who would guess that from these narrow precincts the spirit which new-created Scotland passed away? Or, sailing along the deep, what is there to tell you that this rock was the cage of the captured eagle, the basaltic prison where he chafed and pined and died; and yon, the willow-tree, under which he quietly slept, the Magor-Missabib of modern history? Or, floating on the soft Ægean, and looking up to the marble cliffs, where the aconite grows and the halcyon slumbers in the sun, what trace is there to tell that heaven's windows once opened here; that here the last thrill of inspiration was felt, and here the last glimpse of a glorified Redeemer vouchsafed? To the passing glance or the uninstructed eye, they are mean and inconspicuous places—so mean, that ascertaining the wonders connected with them, the vulgar world declares them unworthy of such distinction till otherwise distinguished, and exclaims, "Let us build a monument, a mausoleum, or a church." But to spirits truly great, every place is great which mind or moral glory has aggrandized. Patmos could not be improved though it were expanded into a continent; nor the house where a poet was born or a Reformer died, though it were enshrined beneath a national monument.

There is another remark which we may make regarding memorable places. They are usually more interesting to strangers than to the regular residents. Had the Esquimaux seen Captain Ross and his party, they would have marvelled what brought a band of Englishmen from their comfortable homes to that bleak and barren shore. And, far from sympathizing in their errand, they could hardly have been taught to understand it. Food, not information, being their chief motive to exertion, they would gladly have sold the magnetic pole for a few pounds of blubber or a few pints of oil. It was interesting enough to British science to bring many at the peril of their lives; but to the poor benighted natives it never had occurred that there was anything more important in that particular spot than in any other bend of their frozen beach. And so of historic scenes. You know more about Luther's bold appearance at the Imperial Diet than do most of the people who now reside at Worms. The spot where a great battle was fought, or where a great hero breathed his last, is often interesting to its inhabitants only as a source of gain; and unless they be men of congenial taste and strong emotion, people will hurry daily past the places consecrated by departed greatness, without finding their step detained or their spirit stirred. It is reserved for the far-come traveller to stand still and wonder where the incurious native trudges on, or only wonders what it is that the stranger is gazing at.

Our earth is a little world. In bulk it is little as compared with some of its neighbors. Even the same planetary system contains one world a hundred times, and another three hundred times as large; whilst, if suns be peopled worlds, there are suns hundreds of thousands of times as large. And there are races of intelligence and capacity far beyond our own—races both fallen and unfallen, to which our highest genius may seem a curious simplicity, and our vastest information an interesting ignorance, even as we may smile at the wit and knowledge of the Esquimaux. But this is the little world, and ours the lowly race, which God selected as the scene and the subject of the most amazing interposition. Like its own Bethlehem Ephratah, little among thousands of worlds; like its own Patmos, a point in the ocean of existence, our earth already stands alone in the universe, and will stand forth in the annals of eternity, illustrious for its fact without a parallel. It is the world on which the mystery of redemption was transacted; it is the world into which Christ came. And though lower than the angels, ours is the race which Jehovah has crowned with one peerless glory, one unequalled honor. It is the race which God has visited. Ours is the flesh which Incarnate Deity wore, and ours is the race for whose sinners the Son of God poured forth a ransom in his blood. This is the event which over our small planet sheds a solemn interest, and draws toward it the wondering gaze of other worlds. And just as in traversing the deep, when there rises on the view some spot of awful interest or affecting memory, you slack the sail, and passengers strain the eye, and look on in silent reverence; so, in their journeys through immensity the flight of highest intelligences falters into wonder and delay as they near this little globe. There is something in it which makes them feel like Moses at Horeb, "Let me draw near and see this great sight,"—a marvel and a mystery here which angels desire to look into. It is a little world, but it is the world where God was manifest in flesh. And though there may be spots round which the interest gathers in most touching intensity; though it may be possible to visit the very land whose acres were trod by "those blessed feet which our offences nailed to the accursed tree;" though you might like to look on David's town where the advent took place, and on the hills of Galilee where his sermons were preached, and on the limpid Gennesareth which once kissed his buoyant sandals, and on that Jerusalem which He loved and pitied, and where He died, and that Olivet, from whose gentle slope the Prince of Peace ascended, I own that with me it is not so much Jerusalem or Palestine as Earth, Earth herself. Since it received the visit of the Son of God, in the eye of the universe the entire globe is a

Holy Land; and such let it ever be to me. So wicked and sin-tainted that it must pass through the fire ere all be ended, it is withal so consecrated and so dear to heaven that it must not be destroyed; but a new earth with righteousness dwelling in it shall perpetuate to distant ages its own amazing story. And though an illustrious author wrote, "I have long lost all attachment to this world as a locality,"* I do not wish to share the feeling. I like it for its very littleness. I like to stand on its lonely remoteness, and look aloft to vaster and brighter orbs; and when I consider the heavens, the moon and the stars, then say I, "What is man that thou shouldest visit him?" And, as in the voyage of the spheres, I sail away in this, the little barque of man, it comes over me with melting surprise and adoring astonishment that mine is the very world into which the Saviour came; and as I farther recall who that Saviour was,—that for Him to become the highest seraph would have been an infinite descent, or to inhabit the

* Foster.

hugest globe a strange captivity,—instead of seeking to inflate this tiny ball into the mightiest sphere, or stilt up this feeble race to angelic stature, I see many a reason why, if an Incarnation were at all to be, a little world should be the theatre, and a little race the object.

It would indeed give melancholy force to the saying, "Much wisdom is much grief," if much wisdom were fatal to the Christian faith, and if he who increased his general knowledge must forfeit his religious hopes. But whilst science is fatal to superstition,—whilst fatal to lying wonders and monkish legends, it is fortification to a scriptural faith. The Bible is the bravest of books. Coming from God, and conscious of nothing but God's truth, it awaits the progress of knowledge with calm security. It watches the antiquary ransacking among classic ruins, and rejoices in every medal he discovers, and every inscription he deciphers; for from that rusty coin or corroded marble it expects nothing but confirmations of its own veracity. In the unlocking of an Egyptian hieroglyphic, or the unearthing of some ancient implement, it hails the resurrection of so many witnesses; and with sparkling elation it follows the botanist as he scales Mount Lebanon, or the zoologist as he makes acquaintance with the beasts of the Syrian desert, or the traveller as he stumbles on a long-lost Petra, or Nineveh, or Babylon; for in regions like these every stroke of the hammer and every crack of the rifle awaken friendly echoes, and every production and every relic bring home a friendly evidence. And from the march of time it fears no evil, but calmly abides the fulfilment of those prophecies and the forthcoming of those events with whose predicted story Inspiration has already inscribed its page. It is not light but darkness which the Bible deprecates; and if men of piety were also men of science, and if men of science would "search the Scriptures," there would be more faith in the earth, and also more philosophy.

Few minds are sufficiently catholic. The

psychologist is apt to despise the material sciences, and few mathematicians are good historians. But although there may be indiffer ence, or rivalry amongst their votaries, there is no antagonism between the truths them selves. There exists a mind as well as a material universe, and there are laws of thought as well as laws of motion; and although it cannot be proved by algebra, yet it is pretty certain that Julius Cæsar invaded Britain, and that George Washington achieved the independence of America. All truths are friendly and mutually consistent, and he is the wisest man who, if he cannot be an adept in all knowledge, dreads none and despises none; the Baconian intelligence to which the Word and the works of the Most High are alike a revelation, and to which both alike are faithful witnesses, though both are not alike articulate.

Be sages then, not sciolists. In the world of knowledge be cosmopolite, and be not the pedants of one department. Be historians as well as mathematicians. Receive every truth on its appropriate evidence, and there is nothing to prevent your faith in the Gospel from being equally strong with your faith in the course of nature. And although the Cyclops of science may have an eye for only one half of truth's horizon; although the bigot of demonstration may jeer at testimony; although the sectary of physics may repudiate history; if your knowledge be really "general;" if it be sufficiently comprehensive and catholic, and correct withal,—the more you grow in knowledge the more will you be confirmed in that most excellent of all knowledge,—a positive and historical Christianity.*

But you say, the natural sciences are all

* Of how much skepticism has Bacon given the rationale in his noted sentence, "A little philosophy inclineth man's mind to Atheism; but depth in philosophy bringeth men's minds about to religion."—ESSAYS 16. And of how many Freethinkers might the foolish boasting be silenced in the words which Newton retorted on the infidel Halley, "I have studied these things, and you have not." There are various sources of unbelief; but next to the "evil heart," the most fruitful is ignorance. It is easy for a sciolist to be a skeptic; but it is not easy for a well-informed historian to reject the records of faith.

certain; theology is all conflict and confusion. Let us understand one another. If you say that the phenomena of nature are all patient and explicit, I reply, And so are the sayings of Scripture. If candor and ingenuousness can interpret the one, they may equally expound the other. But if you say that, unlike the Word of God, his works have never been misunderstood, you surely forget that the "History of the Inductive Sciences" is just a history of erroneous interpretations replaced by interpretations less erroneous, and destined to be succeeded by interpretations still more exhaustive and true. If you smile at the Hutchisonian or Cocceian systems of exegesis; if you quote the hostile theories which still linger in the field of polemics, I ask, Is this peculiar to theology? Have you forgotten how the abhorrers of a vacuum abhorred Torricelli and Pascal? Have you forgotten how the old physiologists were vexed at Harvey for discovering the circulation of the blood? Do you not remember how the Stahlian chemists, like a burnt-out family, long lingered round the ashes of phlogiston, and denounced the wilful fire-raising of Lavoisier and oxygen? In early youth have you never seen a disciple of Werner, and pitied the affectionate tenacity with which he clung to the last plank of the Neptunian theory? Or would every world-maker forgive Lord Rosse's telescope if it swept from the firmament all trace of the nebular hypothesis? Or, because there is still an emission as well as an undulatory theory of light, must we deny that optics is a science, and must we hold that the laws of refraction and reflection are mere matters of opinion? Nature is no liar, although her "minister and interpreter" has often mistaken her meaning; and, notwithstanding the errors which have received a temporary sanction from the learned, there is, after all, nothing but truth in the material universe; and, so far as man has sagacity or sincerity to collect that truth, he has got a true science, a true astronomy, a true chemistry, a true physiology, as the case may be. And even so, whatsoever vagaries particular persons may indulge, or whatsoever false systems may receive a transient support, there is, after all, nothing but truth in the Bible, and so far as we have sincerity or sagacity to collect that Bible-truth, we have got a true religion. Nay, the most important facts and statements in that Word speak for themselves and require no theory. And just as the mariner might safely avail himself of Jupiter's satellites, though Copernicus had never existed; just as the gunner must allow for the earth's attraction, whatever becomes of the Newtonian philosophy; just as the apothecary would continue to mix his salts and acids in definite proportions, even although some mishap befel the atomic theory; just as we ourselves do not close our eyes and dispense with light, until the partisans of rays shall have made it up with the advocates of ether,—so the Scriptures abound in statements and facts on which we may safely proceed, whatever becomes of human theories. "God so loved the world, that He gave his only-begotten Son, that whosoever believeth in Him should not perish, but have everlasting life." "This is a faithful saying, and worthy of all acceptation, that Christ Jesus came into the world to save sinners." "Believe on the Lord Jesus Christ, and thou shalt be saved." "If any man be in Christ Jesus, he is a new creature:" so far as it is founded on such sayings as these, religion is not only the simplest, but, being immediately from God, it is the most secure of all the sciences.

However, we must add one remark. In the region of revealed truth, increasing knowledge will not always be increasing conviction, unless that knowledge be progressively reduced to practice. If knowledge be merely speculative, in extending it a man may only "increase sorrow;" for it is "with the heart that man believeth unto righteousness," and it is to the "doers" of his Father's will that the Saviour promises an assuring knowledge of his own "doctrine."* The mind needs tonics. For the body, next to wholesome food, the best toning is vigorous exercise; and if long cradled in a luxurious repose, the penalty is paid

* Rom. x. 10; John vii. 17.

at last in so many imaginary ills as constitute a real one. And just as the child of sloth is haunted by visionary fears; as he dreads that his pulse will stop or the firmament fall in: so the man who arrests his moral activities and lets his fancy wander at its will; the man who is doing no service to God and no good in the world, will soon become an intellectual hypochondriac. Musing, day-dreaming, marvelling, he will soon believe the phantoms of his own creating, and will not be able to believe the facts of God's revealing. And as the meet recompense of his indolence and uselessness, if he be not given up to believe a lie, his relaxed and pithless grasp will not be able to hold fast a single truth: like an interesting scholar, whose life we lately read, and who during years of speculative inactivity, dwindled down from a devout and laborious clergyman to a slipshod and etiolated free-thinker,* and like those voluptuous theologians of Germany who mope away their lives in selfish

* See the remarks at the close of Archdeacon Hare's "Life of Sterling."

meditation, and who, never letting their brethren taste the fruits of their practical beneficence, are never themselves permitted to taste the blessing of a sure belief. The true remedy for this spiritual moodiness is a holy and abundant activity. So deemed the Apostle Paul. In the midst of a glowing argument, and when refuting certain cavils against the Resurrection which had arisen in the Church of Corinth, he ejaculates all at once, "Be not deceived; evil communications corrupt good manners. Awake to righteousness and sin not, for some have not the knowledge of God."* Like a sagacious physician who finds his patient haunted by fantastic fears, and who orders him out into the open air, and compels him to dig, or row, or wrestle; and after a few days of this rough regimen the crystal arm grows flesh and blood; and he who was afraid that the sky might fall and smother him, begins to have faith in the firmament,—so the apostle sounds a *reveillez* in the ear of these drowsy reasoners. 'Awake to righteousness!

* 1 Cor. xv. 33-35.

These doubts and difficulties are the fruits of sloth. They are the hypochondriac fancies which lazy loungers nurse in one another. Evil communications corrupt good manners. Rouse you!—Awake to righteousness. Bestir you in the business of practical Christianity, and these shadows will flee away!' And so to any haunted or unhappy mind here present we give the same advice. Do you admit the Bible to be the Word of God, and yet are you haunted with speculative doubts and evil surmisings as to any of its particular doctrines? Then, awake to righteousness! Your doubts are ridiculous, your fears are unfounded, and each idle hypothesis might be easily refuted. But the real remedy is, not reasoning, but righteousness; not the arguments of others, but your own practical piety. Awake, then, to righteousness. Embody in your conduct your present limited stock of conviction. Try to pray more, or praise more; try to cure the bad temper or the unholy passion; try to do some good to your neighbors: and that very effort will be the cure of some cavils. It will teach you, for one thing, that the heart is desperately wicked, and that if God does not change it, nothing else can. And that discovery will prompt you to prayer, and that prayer will procure an answer, and that answer will deepen your trust in God; and thus item by item your faith will grow exceedingly. Thus, by the corrective of wholesome discipline and by being confronted with realities, your foolish doubts will dissipate; and the doctrine which was incredible to a lazy and dyspeptic intellect, will soon be absorbed and assimilated by a sound understanding, and become the joy and rejoicing of a sanctified soul.'

Alas! for the knowledge which knows no Saviour. Alas! for the science which includes no Gospel. The most erudite of lawyers was Selden. Some days before his death he sent for Archbishop Ussher, and said, "I have surveyed most of the learning that is among the sons of men, and my study is filled with books and manuscripts on various subjects, yet at this moment I can recollect nothing in them all on which I can rest my soul, save one from the sacred Scriptures, which lies much on my spirit. It is this: 'The grace of God that bringeth salvation hath appeared to all men, teaching us, that denying ungodliness and worldly lusts, we should live soberly, righteously, and godly, in this present world; looking for that blessed hope, and the glorious appearing of the great God, and our Saviour Jesus Christ; who gave Himself for us, that He might redeem us from all iniquity, and purify unto Himself a peculiar people, zealous of good works!'" Nor is it only at the close of the pilgrimage that the hope full of immortality is a pearl of great price. Without it, life is so transient that every invention is a melancholy plaything, and the vastest acquirements are a laborious futility. But the student who toils for immortality need never want a motive in his work; and, however sad some of his discoveries may be, the sage who knows the Saviour will always have in his knowledge an overplus of joy.

LECTURE VI.

The Playhouse and the Palace.

READ ECCLES. II. 1–11.

"Go to now, I will prove thee with mirth." . . "I said of laughter, It is mad." . . . "I gave myself to wine, yet acquainting myself with wisdom." . . . "I made me great works." . . . "Then I looked on all the works that my hands had wrought: and, behold, all was vanity and vexation of spirit."

THIS passage describes a mental fever. The writer tells how, by quitting the wholesome climes of piety, his spirit caught a deadly chill, and how, in the morbid excitement which followed, he tossed to and fro, and tried every change,—burning in the breeze, and shivering in the sun,—distracted till he gained his wish, and disgusted to find that what he wished was not the thing he wanted. First mad after wisdom, then came a surfeit of learning—a glut of information, and he denounced much wisdom as much grief. He would try frivolity. He would take things easily, and, as far as might be, cheerily. "Go to now, I will prove thee with mirth; therefore, enjoy pleasure." He would sip the surface of things, and snatch the joys which divert the mind, but which do not fatigue the brain: he would be a wit, a man of humor, a merry monarch. And he was. But his own mirth soon made him melancholy. Like phosphorus on a dead man's face, he felt that it was a trick, a lie; and, like the laugh of a hyena among the tombs, he found that the worldling's frolic can never reanimate the joys which guilt has slain and buried. "I said of laughter, It is mad; and of mirth, What doeth it?" So, after a moody interval, he bethought him how to blend the two. Philosophy by itself had failed, and folly by itself had also failed. But how would it do to combine them?—the sprightly with the grave, the material luxury and the mental vivacity, the wisdom and the wine? Yes; into his ivy-wreath he would twine the laurel, and the flat potions of philosophy he would enliven with social effervescence. "I sought in mine heart to give myself unto wine, (yet acquainting mine heart with wisdom,) and to lay hold on folly, till I might see what was that good for the sons of men, which they should do under the heaven all the days of their life." But this also proved a failure. "Wine, wisdom, wit," became a mutually destructive mixture, and the experimenter abjured them, in order to try the pleasures of taste. Sculpture and painting were scarcely known to the Hebrews; but in gardening, music, and architecture, they were good proficients, and to these the sovereign now directed his sumptuous ingenuity. Like a petrified dream, the palace stood forth in all the freshness of virgin marble, and in all the pride of its airy pinnacles. In the wilderness waters brake forth, and spreading their molten coolness over the dust of yesterday, artificial lakes surrounded artificial isles; whilst from the fragrant thickets of the terraced gardens, the dulcet sounds of foreign minstrelsy descended where the royal barge lay floating, or through the lattice wafted into the banquet-hall their hints of superhuman glory,—till the vessels of gold and silver sparkled like a galaxy, and the repast was enchanted into a Divine refection; and in proud apotheosis the monarch smiled upon his guests from a godlike throne. "I builded me houses, I planted me vineyards, I made me pools of water to water the groves of trees. I gat me men singers and women singers, and musical instruments of every sort. And whatsoever mine eyes desired I kept not from them; I withheld not my heart from any joy. Then I looked on all the works that I had wrought, and on the labor that I had labored to do; and, behold, all was vanity and vexation of spirit, and there was no profit under the sun."

Solomon tried mirth and abjured it. And, perhaps, the most melancholy life is that of the professed merrymaker. You remember the answer of the wobegone stranger, when the physician advised him to go and hear the great comedian of the day—"You should go and hear Matthews." "Alas! Sir, I am Matthews!" Akin to which is the account of one who for many years manufactured mirth for the great metropolis, the writer of diverting stories, and the soul of every festive party which was able to secure his presence.* But even when keeping all the company in a blaze of hilarity, his own heart was broken; and at one of these boisterous scenes, glimpsing his own pale visage in the glass, he exclaimed, "Ah! I see how it is. I look just as I am—done up in mind, in body, and purse,"—and went home to sicken and die. And who can read this passage without recalling one who was sixty years ago the most dazzling speaker in our British Parliament, whose bow had as many strings as life had pleasures,—the wit, the orator, the dramatist, the statesman, the boon companion and the confidant of princes?† But when "wine" had quenched the "wisdom;" when riot had bloated the countenance, and debt had dispersed the friends of the man of pleasure; when in splendid rows his books

* Theodore Hook. † Richard Brinsley Sheridan.

stood on the shelves of the brokers, and the very portrait of his wife had disappeared,—on a wretched pallet, trembling for fear of a prison, the gloomy, forsaken worldling closed his eyes on a scene which he was loth to quit, but which showed no wish to detain him—leaving "no profit under the sun," and without any prospect beyond it.

Nor can we promise a satisfaction more solid to the godless virtuoso. Every other year the public is startled with some grand explosion. A great tower of Babel comes toppling down. There is a tinkle in the belfry,—a premonitory jangling of the crazy chimes,—a crackling of the timbers, a thunderous down-pouring of bricks and beams and tiles and plaster, and through the dust and smoke the groans of the crushed inmates are heard, stifled and soon stilled: and then come the excavators,—the collectors who carry off the curiosities to decorate other toy-shops, and the builders who buy the bricks, in order to construct new Babels elsewhere.

Not long ago a wealthy compatriot erected

such a palace for his pride, and reared it with such impatience that the workmen plied their labors night and day. When finished, "a wall nearly twenty miles in circumference, surrounded it. Within this circle scarcely any visitors were allowed to pass. In sullen grandeur the owner dwelt alone, shunning converse with the world around. Majesty itself was desirous of visiting this wonderful domain, but was refused admittance. . . . Its interior was fitted with all the splendor which art and wealth could create. Gold and silver cups and vases were so numerous that they dazzled the eye; and looking round at the cabinets and candelabra and ornaments which decorated the apartment, was like standing in the treasury of an Eastern prince."* But a hundred thousand pounds a-year failed to support this magnificence, and the gates which "refused admittance to a monarch were thrust open by a Sheriff's officer:" and whilst its architect pined in unpitied solitude, the gorgeous structure was pulled down by its new owner. More fre-

* "The Mirage of Life," a publication of the Tract Society.

quently, however, it is the structure which stands, and it is the architect who becomes the ruin. Many of you have visited Versailles. As you stood upon its terraces, or surveyed its pictures furlong after furlong, or wandered among its enchanted fountains, did it strike you, How fresh and splendid is Versailles; how insignificant is now its author! Or did you think of that gloomy day when in one of its chambers lay dying the monarch who has identified Versailles with his royal revelries, and near the silken couch a throng of courtiers lingered, not in tears,—not anxious to detain his spirit, not sedulous to soothe the last moments of mortal anguish; but wearying till their old master would make an end of it and die, that they might rush away and congratulate his son and successor.* And did you think that thus it is with every one who layeth up treasure for himself, and who is not rich towards God? Did you think of him who said to his soul, when he had built his larger

* See the death-scene of Louis XV. at the opening of Carlyle's "French Revolution."

barns, "Soul, thou hast goods laid up for many years; take thine ease, eat, drink, and be merry;" and to whom God said, "Thou fool, this night shall thy soul be required of thee: then, whose shall these things be?"

What is it then? Shall we denounce learning, genius, wit? Shall we proscribe architecture and all the arts? For this some have contended, and under pretence of piety they have sought to become barbarians. But, O man, who hath required this at thy hands? It is the work of God's Spirit to sanctify taste and consecrate talent; and that alone is excessive which is not given to God. In "walking about Zion," we must ever admire the noble "bulwarks" reared by Lardner and Butler, and the other defenders of the common faith, as well as the "towers" of orthodoxy erected by the learned labors of Owen, and Haldane, and Magee, and other mighty engineers; nor less the "palaces" which at once adorn the city and commemorate the genius of Watts, and Howe, and Chalmers, and Vinet. Nor is there any reason why wit should always be "mad." Religion may be sprightly, and dulness may be undevout. A Horne or a Cowper may be permitted to answer a fool according to his folly; and when, with the tender precision of a Tell, the polished shafts of Wilberforce split in twain an opponent's argument, but never "hurt his head,"* you could not wish fanaticism to destroy a weapon which religion guides so wisely. Though pride may be the busiest architect, let us not forget that piety and philanthropy have been great builders also. And though sensuality may abuse the arts, let us not forget how often to its youthful inmates music has helped to endear the earthly home, and how much devotion is indebted to "the service of song in the house of the Lord." Let us not forget that almighty Artist who, every spring, paints new landscapes on the earth, and every evening new ones in the sky,—whose sculptures are the melting clouds and everlasting hills,—and whose harp of countless strings includes each

* Ps. cxli. 5. See the sketch of Wilberforce, in Sir James Stephen's "Historical Essays," and in Lord Brougham's "Statesmen," first series.

note from a hare-bell's tinkle to the "organic swell" of ocean's thunder.

What is it then? The "instrument of righteousness" when not "yielded to God," becomes an idol; and every idol is at once a curse and a crime.

LECTURE VII.

The Monument.

READ ECCLES. II. 12–23.

"There is no perpetual remembrance of the wise more than of the fool." "Who knoweth whether his successor shall be a wise man or a fool?"

THE noblest renown is posthumous fame; and the most refined ambition is the desire of such fame. A vulgar mind may thirst for immediate popularity; and very moderate talent, dexterously managed, may win for the moment the hosannas of the million. But it is a Horace or a Milton, a Socrates or a Sidney, who can listen without bitterness to plaudits heaped on feebler rivals, and calmly anticipate the day when posterity will do justice to the powers or the achievements of which he is already conscious. And of this more exalted ambition it would appear that Solomon had felt the stirrings. When he looked on the temple and the cedar palace, and still more when he thought of his literary exploits, his songs and his proverbs, and his lectures in science, the *Non omnis moriar* was a thought as natural as it was pleasing, and from the sense of flagging powers and the sight of a failing body, he gladly took refuge in the promise of posthumous immortality. But even that cold comfort was entirely frozen in the thought which followed. From the lofty pinnacle to which, as a philosophic historian, he had ascended, Solomon could look down and see not only the fallibility of his coevals, but the forgetfulness of the generations following. He knew that there had often been great men in the world; but he could not hide it from himself, how little these great men had grown already, and how infinitesimal the greatest would become, if the world should only last a few centuries longer. And so far, Solomon was right. Few things would be more pathetic than if we had some micrometer for measuring great men's memories,—some means for ascertaining the decimal of a second which those great names subtend in our historic firmament, who filled their living age with lustre. Even Solomon's own, —intellectually the brightest of a bygone dispensation, and with all the advantage of the Bible telescope to bring it near,—how little it enters into the actual thought of this modern world! What a tiny spark it twinkles through the foggy atmosphere of this material time! Had a life in the hearts of future men been all his immortality, how little worth the purchase! and how much wiser than their philosophic monarch were those "fools" in Jerusalem who took no thought to add this cubit to their age!

So, brethren, it is natural to wish to be remembered when gone; and as a substitute for the highest motive, or a succor to other motives, it is well to think of the generation following. But, as it usually flatters worldly men, this posthumous fame is a fallacy.* "A

* "Are not all things born to be forgotten? In truth, it was a sore vexation to me when I saw, as the wise man saw of old, that whatever I could hope to perform must necessarily be of very temporary duration; and if so, why do it?

living dog is better than a dead lion." Amidst the importunate solicitations of daily business, many of us must accuse ourselves of unfaithfulness to the dead; and when tranquil moments call up their familiar images, we marvel how we can deal so treacherously with the great and good departed. Vanished from our view, expunged from our correspondence, dropped from our very prayers, no longer expected as visitors in our homes,—it is marvellous how faint and intermitting their memory has grown; and we upbraid our ungrateful fancy that it preserves so little space for old benefactors, and the once-cherished friends of our bosom. But the same fate awaits ourselves; we, too, are going hence, and when we are gone,

> "A few will weep a little while,
> Then bless our memory with a smile."

Let me see! What have I done already? I have learnt Welsh, and have translated the songs of Ab Gwilym; I have also rendered the old book of Danish ballads into English metre. Good! Have I done enough to secure myself a reputation of a thousand years? Well, but what's a thousand years after all, or twice a thousand years? Woe is me! I may just as well sit still."—LAVENGRO.

One or two may cling to it with tender fondness, while existence lasts; but even with friends affectionate and true, tenderness will soon soften into resignation, and resignation will subside into contentment, and contentment will dull away into sheer forgetfulness; and it will only be on some rare occasion,—some wakeful night, when memory is holding a vigil of all-souls, or when a torn letter, or an inscription in a book, or a name carved on the beechen tree conjures up the past, "and a spirit stands before you," that the fountain of early love will flow anew, and you will pay the tribute of the long-suspended tear. But even that will end. A race will arise that know not Joseph, and to whom Joseph's friends will not be able to transfer their attachment; and when a fourth or a fifth generation comes upon the stage, so dim will be the name, and so diluted will be the interest in it, that the youth would be more concerned for the loss of a favorite hound than for the extinction of his grandsire's memory.

But if this be the phantom for which the

worldling toils and sighs, there is a posthumous fame which is no illusion. If there be no eternal remembrance of the world's wise men any more than of its fools, it is otherwise with the wise ones of the heavenly kingdom. God has so arranged it that "the righteous shall be held in everlasting remembrance." "They that," in his sight, "are wise, shall shine as the firmament, and they that turn many to righteousness, as the stars forever and ever." Great men may covet admiration, but good men crave affection. Admiration is the state-room, formal and rarely used; but to be admitted into the affections is to be domiciled in the heart's own home,—to live where lives the soul itself. And into this inmost shrine of good men's souls God admits all the holy; nay, with reverence speaking it, He admits them into his own. The love of Jehovah is a sanctuary where every holy being has a home. But not content with giving to the just made perfect, the immortality of his own unchanging love, a gracious God secures them the attachment of congenial minds; and at this instant there is not in all the universe a holy being but God has found for it a resting-place in the love of other holy beings, and that not temporarily, but for all eternity. The only posthumous fame that is truly permanent is the memory of God; and the only deathless names are theirs for whose living persons He has found a place in his own love, and in the love of holy beings like-minded with Himself. Many a casket has been broken, and the gems of fine fancy have been scattered on the world, and the name of the self-immolating genius is now forgotten; but that box of ointment which the weeping penitent crushed over the feet of Jesus, will pour its fragrance through all time; for wherever there is a Gospel the Lord Jesus has secured that there shall be spread the story. And so—war, wisdom, wit, —these three have all made deep indentations on the mind of man; and some deeds have been so brave, and some inventions so beautiful, and some sayings so brilliant, that people vowed they never would be forgotten. But, alas! it was the fragile imagination of sinful man, and it has long ago disintegrated. It was the soft and viscid memory of selfish man, and new interests and new objects have since flowed in and filled up the oozy record. But although we dare not say that any thought of earth is so sublime as to merit a record in heaven, on the highest authority we know that no act of faith is so insignificant but it secures a registration there. And although, fearful of posthumous flattery, the dying Howards of our species may direct, "Place a sun-dial on my grave, and let me be forgotten,"—they cannot expunge their labors of love from the book of remembrance, and they will never be forgotten by God.

But even beyond posthumous fame, most men would like to be perpetuated in well-doing and affectionate children. And here again, a gloomy foreboding darkened the mind of Solomon. He had greatly extended his hereditary kingdom; he had amassed an unprecedented fortune; he had built such palaces as only Eastern extravagance had dared to dream; he had covered his name with glory as a statesman and a lawgiver and a sage; and all this glory—these palaces,—yon piles of treasure,—that splendid empire,—the whole was such a prize that if he felt sadness in leaving it, he also felt anxiety about transmitting it. He had a son; but, from expressions here escaping, it would almost seem as if Rehoboam already betrayed the senselessness and arrogance which were afterwards to make him the detestation of his subjects, and the butt of his neighbors. The heathen marriages and the on-goings of the father, at once unkingly and ungodly, were destined to yield their bitter fruits in the son; and it is possible that the backslider already felt punished in foreseeing all the mischief coming on the kingdom through the pride and the blunders of this wayward youth. "Yea, I hated all my labor which I had taken under the sun; because I should leave it unto the man that shall be after me. And who knoweth whether he shall be a wise man or a fool? Yet shall he have rule over all my labor wherein I have labored, and wherein I have showed myself wise under the sun. This also is vanity."

Let those be very thankful who feel that they are better off than Solomon. You have not a sceptre, a title, a vast, income to bequeath; but you have well-doing children. By their industry and mutual affection, above all, by promising appearances of her personal piety, you are encouraged to hope that those who come after you will be an honor to your name. What a mercy! Solomon would have given his sceptre in exchange for your son. But why should not this mercy be yet more frequent? It is true that "grace does not run in the blood, though sin does." But it is also true that God makes his grace more gracious by often causing it to run in the channel of the natural affections. "The promise is unto you, and to your children." And where there is a pious affection, the best gifts will be those we shall covet most earnestly for its objects. Where parental affection is also devout, it will prompt the prayer which David offered at once for himself and for Solomon: "Give the king

Thy judgments, O God, and Thy righteousness unto the king's son." And in that pious affection the Lord sympathizes, and such parental intercessions He delights to hear.

And although, when we think what sort of life Solomon for a long period led; when we reflect that Rehoboam's boyhood and youth were spent in the lap of luxury, and amidst scenes of the most extravagant revelry; when we consider that a polygamist like Solomon can never have a home, and a child like Rehoboam can have no such playmates as are found in an undivided family; when we recall the idolatry and impiety to which his early years had been inured, and remember how bad was the example which his own father had set him—we can scarcely wonder that the son of Solomon proved a heart-break to his father and a stigma on his line: still we are not the less persuaded, that where there is faithfulness to God as well as affection to one's children; where there are earnest prayer and a corresponding pattern; and, especially, where both parents are of one mind, and agreed as touching this thing, God will do it for them, and the promise still hold true, "to you and to your seed after you." The "entail of the covenant" is largely borne out by religious biography, and our Churches are mainly composed of the pious children of Christian parents. Happy they who, instead of a tablet in the churchyard wall, are thus commemorated by polished stones in the living temple!*

* Isaiah liv. 11–13.

LECTURE VIII.

The Clock of Destiny.

READ ECCLES. III. 1–15.

"To everything there is a season." . . . . "In the heart of everything God hath set its era."*

ACCORDING to the mood of the spectator the same phenomena will exert a depressing or a reviving influence; and according to the bias of the reasoner the same facts will be adduced for purposes the most opposite. If we were sure that in this passage Solomon was giving the matured opinion of his latest and penitent life, the text would be a lesson of resignation derived from the absolute sovereignty and all-controlling providence of God; but if, as we have all along held, Solomon writes these

* Vs. 11, עולם eternity, duration, &c. LXX. αιων.

verses somewhat in sympathy with his former self; if he be recalling for wise purposes the reasonings and surmisings of the days of his vanity, we would be prepared to find intermingled with the sublime theology of this section a tincture of fatalism. Accordingly, in the ninth and tenth verses we read, "What profit hath he that worketh in that wherein he laboreth? I have seen the travail which God hath given to the sons of men, to be exercised in it." 'This universe is moving in a groove of adamant. Man's activity is a make-believe, an imposition on himself; for the wheel spins round equally fast whether the blue-bottle push it forward or backward. What profit is there in human industry? It is the unproductive travail to which the offended Creator has doomed his sinful creature;—the ploughing of the sand, the weaving of the air, the manufacture of elaborate nonentities.' And yet, so true are the facts which this section notes, and so solemn the inferences from them which forced themselves on the mind of the royal reasoner, that few texts contain the germs of a grander theology. Passing over the impotence and helplessness of the creature, he saw how glorious was that Omnipotence which held in hand the guiding reins of ponderous orbs and mighty incidents, and at the predestined moment would bring the chariot of his sovereignty to its triumphal goal in the far-off eternity. He saw how vast is that Wisdom which from the beginning had planned the great year of existence, and planned it so complete that nothing needed to be supplemented nor superseded, but through its cycle inconceivable the universe moved on from the moment of its starting, ever waxing, ever waning, and through its summer and winter of uncounted ages circling round to its successive springs. " He hath made everything beautiful in his time, and in the heart of everything He hath set an eternity: so that no man can find out from beginning to end any work that God maketh—any process that God conducteth. I know that whatsoever God doeth, it shall be forever. Nothing can be put to it, nor anything taken from it. That which hath been is now, and that which is to be hath already been: and God brings back the past."

"To everything there is a season, and a time to every purpose under the heaven." As if he had said, Mortality is a huge time-piece wound up by the almighty Maker; and after He has set it a-going nothing can stop it till the angel swears that time shall be no longer. But here it ever vibrates and ever advances,—ticking one child of Adam into existence, and ticking another out. Now it gives the whirr of warning, and the world may look out for some great event; and presently it fulfils its warning, and rings in a noisy revolution. But there! as its index travels on so resolute and tranquil, what tears and raptures attend its progress! It was only another wag of the sleepless pendulum; but it was fraught with destiny, and a fortune was made,—a heart was broken,—an empire fell. We cannot read the writing on the mystic cogs as they are coming slowly up; but each of them is coming on God's errand, and carries in its graven brass a Divine decree. Now, however,—now that the moment is past, we know; and in the fulfilment we can read the fiat. This instant was to say to Solomon, "Be born!" this other was to say to Solomon in all his glory, "Die!" That instant was to "plant" Israel in Palestine; that other was to "pluck him up." And thus inevitable, inexorable, the great clock of human destiny moves on, till a mighty hand shall grasp its heart and hush forever its pulse of iron.

See how fixed, how fated is each vicissitude! how independent of human control! There is "a time to be born," and however much a man may dislike the era on which his existence is cast, he cannot help himself: that time is his, and he must make the most of it. Milton need not complain that his lot is fallen on evil days; for these are *his* days, and he can have no other. Roger Bacon and Galileo need not grudge their precious being, that they have been prematurely launched into the age of inquisitors and knowledge-quenching monks,—for this age was made to make them. And so with the time to die. Voltaire need not offer half his fortune to buy six weeks' reprieve; for if the appointed moment has arrived it cannot pass into eternity without taking the skeptic with it. And even good Hezekiah—his tears and prayers would not have turned the shadow backward had that moment of threatened death been the moment of God's intention. Yes, there is a time to die; and though we speak of an *un*timely end, no one ever died a moment sooner than God designed, nor lived a moment longer. And so there is a time to plant. The impulse comes on the man of fortune, and he lays out his spacious lawn, and studs it with massive trees; and he plants his garden, and in the sod imbeds the rarest and richest flowers, or he piles up little mounts of blossomed shrubbery, till the place is dazzled with bright tints and dizzy with perfume. And that impulse fades away, and in the fickleness of sated opulence the whole is rooted up, and converted into wilderness again. Or by his own or a successor's fall, the region is doomed to destruction; and when strangling nettles have choked the geraniums and the lilies, and, crowded into atrophy, the lean plantations grow tall and branchless, the axe of an enterprising purchaser clears the dank thickets away, and his ploughshare turns up the weedy parterre. There is a time when to interfere with disease is to destroy; when to touch the patient is to take his life: and there is a time when the simplest medicine will effect a marvellous cure. There is a time when the invader is too happy to dismantle the fortress which so long kept him at bay; but by-and-by, when he needs it as a bulwark to his own frontiers, with might and main he seeks to build it up again. Nor can any one fix a date and say, I shall spend that day merrily, or I must spend it mournfully. The day fixed for the wedding may prove the day for the funeral; and the ship which was to bring back the absent brother, may only bring his coffin. On the other hand, the day we had destined for mourning, God may turn to dancing, and may gird it with irresistible gladness. Nor are earth's monuments perpetual. The statue reared one day will be thrown into the river another, and the trophy commenced by one conqueror shall owe its completion to his rival and supplanter. "There is a time to embrace, and a time to refrain from embracing." "There is a time when the fondness of friendship bestows its caresses, and receives them in return with reciprocal sincerity and delight; and a time when the ardor cools; when professions fail; when the friend of our bosom's love proves false and hollow-hearted, and the sight of him produces only the sigh and tear of bitter recollection. We refrain from embracing, because our embrace is not returned."* "There is a time to get, and a time to lose." There is a time when every enterprise succeeds; when, as if he were a Midas, whatsoever the prosperous merchant touches, is instantly gold; then comes a time when all is adverse,—when flotillas sink, when ports are closed, and each fine opening only proves another and a tantalizing failure. And so there is "a time to keep, and a time to cast away." There is a time when in the cutting

* Wardlaw *in loco.*

blast the traveller is fain to wrap his cloak more closely round him; a time when in the torrid beam he is thankful to be rid of it. There is a time when we cannot keep too carefully the scrip or satchel which contains the provision for our journey; a time when to outstrip the pursuing assassin, or to bribe the red-armed robber, we fling it down without a scruple. It was a time to keep when the sea was smooth, and Rome's ready market was waiting for the corn of Egypt; but it was a time to cast the wheat into the sea, when the angry ocean clamored for the lives of thrice a hundred passengers.* There is "a time to rend, and a time to sew:" a time when calamity threatens or grief has come, and we feel constrained to rend our apparel and betoken our inward woe; a time when the peril has withdrawn, or the fast is succeeded by a festival, when it is equally congruous to remove the symbols of sorrow. There is a time to keep silence—a time when we see that our neighbor's grief is great, and we will not sing songs

* Acts xxvii. 38.

to a heavy heart;—a time when, in the abatement of anguish, a word of sympathy may prove a word in season;—a time when to remonstrate with the transgressor, would be to reprove a madman, or, like the pouring of vinegar on nitre, would be to excite a fiery explosion against ourselves; but a time will come when, in the dawn of repentance or the sobering down of passion, he will feel that faithful are the wounds of a friend. "There is a time to love and a time to hate." There is a period when, from identity of pursuit, or from the spell of some peculiar attraction, a friend is our all in all, and our idolatrous spirits live and move and have their being in him; but with riper years or changing character, the spell dissolves, and we marvel at ourselves that we could ever find zest in insipidity or fascination in vulgarity. And just as individuals cannot control their hatred and their love; as the soul must go forth to what is amiable, and revolt from what is odious,—so nations cannot regulate their pacifications and their conflicts. But just at the moment when they are pledging a perpetual alliance, an apple of discord is thrown in, and to avenge an insulted flag, or settle a disputed boundary, or maintain the tottering balance of power, wager of battle is forthwith joined; and where early summer saw the mingled tribes tilting in the tournay, or masquerading on the fields of cloth of gold, autumn sets on unreaped harvests, and blackened forests, and silent villages. And conversely: when the clouds of battle frown on one another, and there is no prospect but long and sanguinary campaigns, a magazine explodes, an heir-apparent dies, or two daring spirits of the opposing hosts transfer the issue to the point of their single swords; and with the awful incubus so suddenly thrown off, the knit brows of either nation relax into an expansive smile, and the year destined for mutual extermination is spent in blended jubilee.

Such is the fact. Such are the unquestionable alternations in human affairs; and thus accurately do occasions and events fit one another. So much of mechanism does there appear to be in the on-goings of mortality and thus helpless seems man as the maker of his own destiny. But lifting our eyes from the mundane side of it, what shall we say concerning Him who is the Contriver and Controller of it all?

And should it not be enough to say that God has so arranged it? To Him are owing all this variety and vicissitude, and yet all this order and uniformity. And is it not enough that He so wills it? Shall the thing formed say to Him who made it, Why hast thou made me thus?

But not only has God made everything, but there is a beauty in this arrangement where all is fortuitous to us, but all is fixed by Him. "He hath made everything beautiful in its time;" and that season must be beautiful which to infinite Love and Wisdom seems the best.

Amongst modern processes one of the most beautiful is the art of taking sun-pictures. Instead of the artist copying the object, he lets the object copy itself; and if the light were profuse enough and properly adjusted, the picture would be as true as noon, and as minute as the original. Now, would not it be a cu rious thing if, from a station high enough, one could take a vast sun-picture of this city,—this island,—this hemisphere?—showing precisely how at the self-same instant all its inhabitants are occupied?—where every one of them is this moment posted, and what each one of them is doing? And would it not be very curious if along with this there were preserved a similar picture of the self-same people and their employments, at a given instant ten or twenty years ago? But most curious of all would it not be, if some one could show a photographic panorama of how it will appear ten or twenty years hereafter?—projecting every person in his proper place?—exhibiting the groups which have meanwhile gathered round him or melted from his side?—the changes which have passed over himself, or which he has been the means of inducing over others? But, my friends, there is one repository where such pictures are preserved,—far more exact and vivid than the finest sun-painting ever drawn; there is not a day in our world's past history but its minutest image lives in the memory of God, and more than that, there is not a day in all the coming history of our world but its portrait precise and clear is already present to the Divine foreknowledge. "Known unto God are all his works from the beginning of the creation;" and so to speak, each day that dawns, though its dawning include an earthquake, a battle, or a deluge,—each day that dawns, however many it surprises, is no surprise to Him who sees the end from the beginning, and who, in each evolving incident, but sees the fulfilment of his "determined counsel,"—the translation into fact of one other omniscient picture of the future.

And which is best? "A mighty maze and all without a plan?"—a world whose progress takes even Providence by surprise, and whose future stands before even the Infinite Mind in no clearer outline than those dim guesses and dusky foreshadowings to which even shrewd mortals attain?—or a world of which the successive epochs shall only be the outworking of a purpose so wise and good from the first that it cannot be changed for the better?—the realization in persons and actions and results of that series of prescient maps or plans whose aggregate will constitute the optimism of the universe?—as we read in verse 11, "God hath set its destined duration in the heart of everything." To every incident or event He has not only given its immediate effect, but also its remoter errand afar in the future. Each such incident or event may be regarded as a mechanism wound up to travel so far or accomplish so much, so that, till its course is finished, till the beginning comes round to the end, no man can say positively what was God's first purpose in it.

When the young German grew earnest, you would have said there was some hope that he might next be enlightened; but when the earnest youth became a monk, you would have said, Farewell, light! farewell, all hope of the Gospel! And yet Luther's entombment in the Erfurth convent was to be the resurrection of apostolical religion. In the heart of that little incident God had set the Reformation. When a king arose in Egypt who knew not Joseph, and who hated and tormented the Hebrews, you would have said, There's an end of the old promise. This order to exterminate the Hebrew children will soon annihilate Abraham's family. And any Jew who had been gathered to his fathers at the time they were slaying all the male-children, would have been apt to die despairing of his nation's prospects. And yet that murderous edict was to be the deliverance of Israel. In the heart of that despot's decree God had set the exodus. And to the sublime theology of Solomon, the only addition we would make is that Evangelic supplement: "All things work together for good to them that love God; to them which are the called according to his purpose." Their path is thickly strewn with incidents. Of these, some are for the present not joyous but grievous: nevertheless in their heart God hath set the peaceful fruits of righteousness. They are seeds with a thorny husk, and they hurt the pilgrim's naked feet; but when next he passes that way, or when Christiana with her children follows him, they have germinated into bright flowers or cool, overshadowing trees. And they will not perish. The incidents along the believer's path are seeds of influence, scattered by the hand of God. And sanctification of some sort is the germ which He has set in the heart of every one of them. Nor can they die till they have thus developed. They cannot perish and pass away till the Christian has set in his heart the lesson which God has set in theirs.

The works of God are distinguished by *opportuneness of development and precision of purpose.* There is a season for each of them, and each comes in its season. All of them have a function to fulfil, and they fulfil it. To which, verse 14, he adds that they are all of their kind *consummate*,—so perfect that no improvement can be made, and, left to themselves, they will be perpetual. "I know that whatsoever God doeth, it shall be forever; nothing can be put to it, nor anything taken from it." How true is this regarding God's greatest work, redemption! What more could he have done to make it a great salvation than what He had already done? or what feature of the glorious plan could we afford to want? And now that He has Himself pronounced it a "finished" work, what is there that man can put to it?—what is there he dare take from it? And in doing it He has done it "forever." The merits of Immanuel are as mighty this evening as they were on the day of Pentecost. Jesus is as able to save us if we come unto God by Him now, as He was to save Zaccheus and Legion, and Mary Magdalene. It is into the same bright heaven that these merits and that mercy will take us as that into which the white-robed company have already gone, and by a process as swift as that which translated the dying thief, these merits could transport any sinner amongst us, from the verge of perdition to Paradise.

Of these theological conclusions the 15th verse is the last. "That which hath been, is now, and that which is to be hath already been, and God requireth,—God resuscitates and repeats the past." There is an *uniformity* in the Divine procedure. True to itself, amidst all the diversity of incidents which chequer an individual's history, there are certain great principles from which Infinite Wisdom never deviates. In the natural world there is always a summer and a winter, a seed-time and a harvest, a day succeeded by the night. And in the moral world sin will always be sorrow; principle will, in the long run, always prove the highest expediency; the sinner will always sooner or later be filled with the fruit of his own devices; and sooner or later there will always be a reward to the righteous. And amidst all the diversities of national character, and all the vicissitudes of civil history, there is an essential identity,—variety enough to spread romantic fascination over the page of Thucydides or Robertson, but such identity that the fifteenth Psalm, or a single section of this book, is the abridgment of all history. Nor will there be any material change till the story is ended. Hundreds of millions may yet be born, but they will all repeat the past. A few may be more clever, and a few may be more virtuous than any that have heretofore been; and alas! a few may be more abandoned, more desperately wicked. But whether for good or evil, they will all be human,—human in their goodness, human in their guilt. There will not be a Gabriel among them all, nor will there be a Lucifer; and in dealing with that humanity the principles of the Divine procedure will be as uniform as the material itself. With the reprobate it will be calls and refusals, warnings and resistings, startling providences and sullen stupor, momentary alarms, followed by deeper slumber; and then, "he who being often reproved, hardeneth his neck, shall suddenly be cut off, and that without remedy;" and, on the other side, the converse process. "Whom He did foreknow He also did predestinate. Moreover, whom He did predestinate, them He also called, and whom He called, them He also justified, and whom He justified, them He also glorified."* And thus, through all the operations of nature, prov-

* Rom. viii. 29, 30.

idence, and grace, "that which hath been, is now, and that which is to be hath already been, and God repeateth that which is past."

One final reflection from the whole passage. Some of you, my hearers, may read the description of mortality here recorded; and you may give a vehement assent to its truth. "Yes, it is all a masquerade of the same everlasting events wearing new vizors; it is all mutation without novelty and change without real variety. The world itself is a gourd whose root the worm is already gnawing,—a palace whose quicksand basis the flood is already sapping.

> "What is this passing scene?
> A peevish April day!
> A little sun, a little rain,
> And then night sweeps along the plain,
> And all things fade away."*

So be it. But if so, how should it endear that state where all is perfection, and all is permanence! To everything "under heaven" there

* Kirke White.

is a fixed but a fleeting season; but to those who are in heaven the moments are not thus precarious, nor the seasons thus short. And still better, there are many of the things for which there is a "time" on earth for which there is no time there. To those who are born into that better country there is no time to "die." Those that are "planted" in God's house on high, shall never be "plucked up," but shall flourish there forever. There, there is nothing to hurt nor to destroy, but perpetual "health," and lasting as eternity. There, the walls of strong salvation shall never be broken down. There, there is no time to weep; for sorrow and sighing are forever fled away: no "time to mourn;" for, when they left this vale of tears the days of their mourning ended. There, it is all a time of "peace," and all a time to love. There, monuments are never defaced nor overthrown; for those who are pillars in the temple above, with the new name written on them, shall go out no more. There, in the sanctity of the all-superseding relationship, there will be no severance; but those friends of earth, who have been joined again in the bonds of angelhood, will never need to give the parting embrace; for they shall be ever with one another, and ever with the Lord.

LECTURE IX.

The Dungeon.

READ ECCLES. III. 16–22; IV. 1–3.

"Behold! the tears of the oppressed!"

WHEN composing himself for a contented life, a shriek of anguish reached the monarch's ear and startled his repose. It was a cry from the victims of tyranny and oppression, and as he listened it grew more articulate, and it filled him at once with sympathy for others, and solicitude for himself. "I saw the place of judgment, that wickedness was there; and the place of righteousness, that iniquity was there. I considered all the oppressions that are done under the sun: and behold the tears of such as were oppressed, and they had no comforter; and on the side of their oppressors there was power;

but they had no comforter." How is it possible for a prince to "eat and drink, and enjoy the fruit of his labor," whilst the wail of evicted peasants and houseless orphans is louder than all the music of his orchestra? For a moment he felt relief in recalling the future judgment. "I said in mine heart, God will judge the righteous and the wicked." But what care they for the judgment? What fear of God is before their eyes? So brutish are they that they neither look forward nor look up; but are content with their daily raven. Yes, beasts, I half believe you. Your grossness almost converts me to your own materialism. I wish that God would manifest you to yourselves, and show you how brutish you are living, and how brute-like you will die. Yes, tyrants and oppressors, you have power at present; but you will fall like the beasts that perish. You and they will all go to one place,—will all resolve into promiscuous clay; for "all are of the dust, and all turn to dust again." And as for your very soul, so unfeeling, so undevout as you have been, what is there to mark your spirit more aspiring, more empyrean, than the downward and dissolving spirit of the beast? No; there are sharks in the ocean, and wolves in the forest, and eagles in the air; and there are tyrants on thrones, and there are tormentors in many a cottage. It is painful to know the misery they are daily inflicting, and, perhaps, I myself may yet become their prey. But they must not spoil this transient life-luxury; they shall not fill me with vain compassion or fantastic fears. After all, there is nothing better than to "rejoice in one's own works," and be, as long as he can, oblivious of surrounding misery,—regulating his own movements and rejoicing in his own resources. "For that is his present portion; and who can reveal the future?" Said I so? Ah! vain resolution and unavailing vow! That cry of tortured innocence is in my ear again. I hear the groans of the victim, and I see the tears of the oppressed. And my heart grows sick, and I wish that I were dead, or rather that I had never been born into a world where all proceeds so sadly.

Very ghastly is the picture which our world presents when we look at it as the scene of injustice and cruelty; and very painful is the view it gives us of our arbitrary and oppressive human nature. Could we only see what God is daily seeing, and hear what God is daily hearing, we would be apt to join with Solomon in praising the dead who are already dead, and who are past our pain or danger. For, even now, in this noon of the nineteenth century, which, in the ear Eternal, is the loudest of earth's voices?—which is the loudest in the ear of History? Is it the psalm of thanksgiving? Is it the harvest hymn of ripe fruition and cheerful prospects? Is it the new song of redeemed and regenerate adoration? What is the speech which day utters unto day, —the watchword which one terrestrial night passes on to another? Alas! it is lamentation and mourning. It is the music of breaking hearts; it is the noise of the oppressor's millstone, whose grinding never waxes low. It is the sighing of the prisoner whom the despot has doomed; the groaning of the victim whom lucre has enslaved, or whom superstition means to immolate. That heavy plunge far out on the moon-lit Bosphorus is the close of one household tragedy; in that sudden shriek and weltering fall on the Venetian pavement ends another. These cries of horror announce the funeral of some Ashanti prince, and the wholesale slaughter which soaks his tomb; whilst from Austrian dungeons and Ural mines, the groans of patriots confess the power of tyrants. And even if the modern surface were silent, History cannot be deaf to the voices underneath. For, wheresoever she sets her foot, there is a stifled sob,—that cry which nothing can deaden or keep down,—the quenchless cry of blood,—blood like Abel's, blood like Stephen's, blood like the Saviour's own; and as if the turf were all one altar, and every pore a several tongue, she hears the slain of centuries invoking heaven's pity,—Bethlehem's innocents, Roman martyrs, Bartholomew's victims; and the ground begins to quake as the muffled chorus waxes louder: "How long, O Lord, holy and true, dost thou not avenge our blood on them that dwell on the earth?"*

There are few deeds of kindness which are not sufficiently notorious,—few acts of munificence or mercy which the world's right hand has not hinted to its left. But when History begins her sterner survey,—when from Popedoms and dynasties, and Republics even, she lifts the gilt and purple canopy,—what sights of paltry vengeance or ingenious cruelty offend the reluctant gaze! What secrets of the prison-house do Bastiles and Inquisitions, San Angelos, and London Towers disclose, as the daylight of inquiry breaks in, and the earthen floor gives up its slain, and the stone wall gives out its skeletons! There are depths of the ocean to which the plummet of the mariner, and the dredge of the naturalist, and the exploring foot of the diver, have never travelled down; but even there, as she takes her telescope, History sees the bones thick strewn of the hapless men whom the buccaneer, and the pirate, and the flying slaver, have flung

* Rev. vi. 9–12.

quick into the deep: and there are dim recesses of old story from which no gleams of humanity or tenderness beam forth; but even thence, by the light of Egyptian brick-kilns, and Druid bale-fires, and Assyrian conflagrations, we are reminded that the anguish of his fellow has always been the amusement of the warrior and the solace of the priest. So that, morally regarded, and taking in the continuous survey of all places and all time, green may be the color of the globe, but red is the livery of man. Babel may have split the dialects of earth into a thousand tongues; but, amidst them all, the old vernacular of anguish still survives. And in the music of the spheres its Maker may have given to our world its proper note; but it is a minor tune which is ever sung by its inhabitants, by neighbor nations, and by the several classes of society, evermore to one another, crying, Woe, woe, woe.

Such oppressions Solomon beheld, and more especially judicial oppressions,—cruelty in the cloak of law (iii. 16)—and from the contemplation his mind sought refuge in the Supreme

Tribunal. "I said in mine heart, God shall judge the righteous and the wicked." And though, in the agitated state of his spirit, the recollection did not long abide, the fact is true and the consolation lasting.

The Lord has a bottle, and into that bottle He puts his people's tears, and the tears of all who are oppressed. When Joseph wept at Dothan, and the Jews at Babylon, it was not the sand of the desert nor the stream of Euphrates which intercepted the tear; but God's bottle. When the poor man works hard, and, coming for his wages, gets only rough words or coarse ridicule; when, from the hapless negro, his wife and children are torn by some vindictive master, and sold into a distant State; when, in her new mourning, the bewildered mother goes to claim the scanty provision for her babes, and finds that a cunning quirk has left her not only a widow, but a pauper,—man may mock the misery, but God regards the crime. And whether it be the scalding tear of the Southern slave, or that which freezes in the Siberian exile's eye, God's bottle has received them all; and when the measure is full, the tears of the oppressed burst in vials of vengeance on the oppressor's head.

So true is this that, whenever it foretells retribution, poetry becomes prophetic:—

> "Ye horrid towers, the abode of broken hearts;
> Ye dungeons, and ye cages of despair,
> That monarchs have supplied from age to age
> With music such as suits their ears,—
> The sighs and groans of miserable men!
> There's not an English heart that would not leap
> To hear that ye were fallen."

So sang the bard of Olney in the hey-day of the Bourbons; and a few years later the heart of England did leap, for the Bastile was fallen. And two centuries have passed sinee, like a Hebrew seer, our Milton prayed:—

> "Avenge, O Lord, thy slaughtered saints, whose bones
> Lie scattered on the Alpine mountains cold."

And there is not a succeeding age which has not seen an instalment of the vengeance; and our own is witnessing that fulfilment which "the triple tyrant" most abhors,—the resurrection of their ashes in Roman Protestants and Italian friends of freedom.

This is a great principle, and not to be lost sight of—the weakness of oppression, the terrible strength of the oppressed. I do not allude to the elasticity of the human heart, though that is very great, and is apt, sooner or later, to heave off despotisms and every sort of incubus. I do not so much allude to that —for elastic though it is, it sometimes has been crushed. But I allude to that all-inspecting and all-adjusting Power which controls the affairs of men. And though Solomon felt so perturbed by the prosperous cruelty he witnessed; though he "beheld the tears of such as were oppressed, and they had no comforter; for on the side of their oppressors there was power;"—had he bent his eye a little longer in the direction where it eventually rested, he would have found a Comforter for the oppressed, and would have seen the impotence of the oppressor. For "God shall judge the righteous and the wicked" (iii. 17), or as the close of the book more amply declares it, "God shall bring every work into judgment, with every secret thing, whether it be good, or whether it be evil." And with two worlds in which to outwork the retribution, and with a whole eternity to overtake the arrears of time, Oh! how tyrants should fear for God's judgments; and that match which themselves have kindled, and which is slowly creeping round to explode their own subjacent mine, in what floods of repentance, if wise, would they drench it! Had they been wise enough to remember that "on the side of the oppressed" there is always infinite "Power," Pharaoh would have dreaded the Hebrew infants more than the Hebrew soldiery, and Herod would have been more frightened for the babes of Bethlehem than for the legions of Rome. To David the most dreadful of foes would have been the murdered Uriah, and to Ahab the hosts of Syria, compared with the corpse of Naboth, need have given no uneasiness. More than all the might of Britain had Napoleon cause to dread the blood of D'Enghien, and, beyond all foreign enemies, should modern nations tremble for their slaves: FOR ON THE SIDE OF THE

OPPRESSED IS OMNIPOTENCE, AND THE MOST DEATHLESS OF FOES IS A VICTIM!

My friends, the Gospel is the law of liberty. Such an antagonist is it to all that is unfair and arbitrary and oppressive, that it is only where there is a reign of darkness that there can be a reign of despotism. Even as it is, every Christian is a freeman. His loyalty to God is liberty. It is freedom from tyrannical lusts and task-master passions. It is the bond of iniquity broken. It is emancipation from the thraldom of Satan. And if there were two countries, one of which the Son of God had made free,* and the other of which had freed itself; in one of which Christians were ruled by an absolute but God-fearing Dictator, and in the other of which the slaves of Satan ruled themselves,—we know very well where we should find the greater freedom. But still, the tendency of the Gospel is to do away the pride and imperiousness and unfairness which are here called "oppression;" and if there were any land where these two truths were

* John viii. 32, 36.

practically realized, "God is Light," and "God is love,"—that land would be a land of liberty.

Still, liberty, or exemption from man's oppression, is a priceless blessing. And it may be worth while to ask, What can Christians do for its culture and diffusion?

And, first of all, yourselves be free. Seek freedom from fierce passions and dark prejudices. If you are led captive by the devil at his will, you are sure to become an oppressor. In the greed of gain you will be apt to defraud the hireling of his wages; and that is oppression. In the fury of affronted pride, you will be apt to wreak disproportionate wrath on the offender; and that also is oppression. In the narrowness of sectarianism you will be ready to punish men for their convictions; and such persecution is oppression. He who governs his family by fear is an oppressor. He who tries to accomplish by force what can be effected by reason, is an oppressor. And if he would only look, such a man might see the tears of those whom he oppresses. He might see the tears of the broked-hearted supplicant who with case unheard and with a rude rebuff, has been driven from his door. He might see the tears of the conscientious laborer who has been deprived of bread and bereft the maintenance for his family by refusing Sunday work. He might see the tears of his dependant who, for attendence on some interdicted place of worship or for adherence to a sect proscribed, has received his warning. And though a tear be a little mirror, did he but behold it for one calm moment, it might reveal the oppressor to himself, and save a multitude of sorrows.

Beware of confounding liberty with license. One of the greatest blessings in a state, or in a Christian Church, is good government; but from mistaken notions of independence, it is the delight of some to "speak evil of dignities." They carp and cavil at every law, and they set at defiance every regulation of the powers that be, and one would almost fancy that in their esteem rulers were ordained as a target for public rancor, or a safety-valve for national spleen. On the other hand, an enlightened Christian and patriot will always remember that a constitutional Government,—a Government where himself and the rulers have given mutual guarantees,—is too great a mercy to be lightly imperilled: and he will also remember that where obedience is order, anarchy is pretty sure to end in oppression. It was a noble sentiment, not only for a soldier but for a subject, "I like to be at my post, doing my duty; indifferent whether one set or another govern, provided they govern well."* And like the hero who originally uttered it, the man who is thus magnanimous in obeying is likely to be mighty in command.

And, finally, cultivate a humane and gentle spirit. Every master, every parent, every public functionary, must, from time to time, pronounce decisions or give commands which cross some one's wishes or derange some one's plans. But it will go far to propitiate compliance when it is seen that it is not in recklessness, but for good reason; or, perhaps, from

* "Life of General Sir John Moore," vol. ii. p. 14.

a regretted necessity that the unwelcome order is given; for where there is tenderness, there never can be tyranny. On the other hand, wherever there is thoughtlessness there will be tyranny; and wherever there is a hard or cruel nature, it only needs that power be added in order to make a Nero.

Here it is that the mollifying religion of Jesus comes in as the great promoter of freedom and the great opponent of oppression. By infusing a benevolent spirit into the bosom of the Christian, it makes him the natural guardian of weakness and the natural friend of innocence. And whether it be the savage sportsman who gloats over the tears and dying shudders of the harmless forest-ranger, or who, shooting the parent-bird on her way to the eyrie, leaves the callow nestlings to pine away with slow hunger;—or the kidnapper who carries off the struggling boy from his mother's arms, or stows away in separate ships bound for far-sundered shores, the young chieftain and his bride;—or the Moslem conqueror who hews his way from land to land through fields of quivering slain;—or the

> "Cowl'd demons of the inquisitorial cell,
> The worse than common fiends from heaven that fell,
> The baser, ranker sprung, Autochthones of hell;"—*

Whichever be the form of oppression which nightmares our sympathies, or the form of cruelty which lacerates our feelings, we foresee an end of it in the final triumph of the cross. We foresee an end of it when the Saviour asserts his rightful supremacy, and subdues all things under Him. "For the earnest expectation of the creature waiteth for the manifestation of the sons of God:" and till then, in every groan of the creature we must recognize a pledge and a prayer that the Son of God will be manifest once more, and that the disciples of Jesus will yet be numerous enough to secure a reign of peace and justice in this sin-cursed world. And as we listen to these inarticulate groans of the burdened creation, we, who are nature's interpreters and the world's

* Coleridge.

intercessors, must translate them into the petition, "Thy kingdom come: Thy will be done on earth as it is in heaven. Even so, come, Lord Jesus."

LECTURE X.

The Sanctuary.

READ ECCLES. v. 1–7.

"Keep thy foot when thou goest to the house of God."

VANITY of vanities: human occupation, human existence is all fantastic and foolish. Verily, each man walketh in a vain show; surely they are disquieted in vain. Like the fly-plague in Egypt, every scene of mortal life is infested by frivolity and falsehood; and it is hard to tell which is the sorest vexation,—the buzz and bewilderment of vanities still living, or the noisomeness of those that are dead. The cottage and the palace, the student's chamber and the prince's banquet-room all teem with them, and there is no secure retreat from those vanities which on the wing are a weariness, and, in the cup of enjoyment, are the poison of pleasure. 'Nay, we have not tried that temple,—we have not yet gone to the house of God. There, perhaps, we shall find a tranquil asylum. There, if anywhere, we should find a heaven on earth,—a refuge from the insincerity and unsatisfactoriness which elsewhere abound.' Ah, no; the temple itself is full of vacant worship. It resounds with rash vows and babbling voices. It is the house of God, but man has made it a nest of triflers, a fair of vanity, a den of thieves. Some come to it as reckless and irreverent as if they were stepping into a neighbor's house. Some come to it and feel as if they laid the Most High under obligation because they bring a sheaf of corn or a pair of pigeons; whilst they never listen to the lessons of God's Word, nor strive after that obedience which is better than sacrifice. Some come and rattle over empty forms of devotion, as if they would be heard because of their much speaking. And some come, and in a fit of fervor utter vows which they forget to pay; and when reminded of their promise by the "angel" of the church,—

the priest or his messenger,—they protest that there must be some mistake; they repudiate the vow, and say "it was an error."

A thoughtless resorting to the sanctuary; inattention and indevotion there; and precipitancy in religious vows and promises, are still as common as in the days of Solomon. And for these evils the only remedy is that which he prescribes,—a heartfelt and abiding reverence. "Fear thou God;" "God is in heaven, and thou upon earth;" "Keep thy foot when thou goest to the house of God."

I. There is a preparation for the sanctuary. Not only should there be prayer beforehand for God's blessing there, but a studious effort to concentrate on its services all our faculties. In the spirit of that significant Oriental usage which drops its sandals at the palace door, the devout worshipper will put off his travel-tarnished shoes,—will try to divest himself of secular anxieties and worldly projects,—when the place where he stands is converted into holy ground by the words, "Let us worship God."

Be "ready to *hear*." We freely grant that

dull hearing is often produced by dull speaking. We allow that there is a great contrast when the sameness of sermons is set over against the variety and vivacity of Scripture. And so often is the text injured by its treatment, that we have often wished that some power could give it back in its original pungency, and divested of its drowsy associations. That passage of the Word was a burning lamp, till the obscuring interpretation conveyed it under a bushel. It was a fire, till a non-conducting intellect encased it, and made it like a furnace in felt. It was the finest of the wheat, till a husky understanding buried it in chaff. It was "a dropping from the honey-comb," till tedious insipidity diffused it and drowned it in its deluge of commonplace. And we allow that much of the impatience and inattention of hearers may be owing to the prolixity of preachers. But still, admitting that on the one side there is often the fault of commonplace as well as "the sin of excessive length,"* and conceding to every

* Bishop Shirley.

hearer the same right to exert his tasteful and intellectual faculties when listening to a sermon as when perusing a printed book; you will not deny that on the other side there are often a langour and lukewarmness of which the cure must be sought not so much in the greater power of the preacher as in the growing piety of the hearer. There are two sorts of instruction to which if we do not hearken we are utterly without excuse. One is the direct instruction of God's Word; the other is truth and earnestness embodied in a Christian teacher. But how often are the lively oracles read in public worship, and a relief experienced when the lesson is ended! and how often does some fervent evangelist pour forth appeals full of that rarest originality,—the pathos of a yearning spirit,—and find no response save stolid apathy, or a patronizing compliment to his energy!

Half the power of preaching lies in the mutual preparation. The minister must not serve God with that which costs him nothing: but it is not the minister alone who should "give attendance to reading, to exhortation, to doctrine." There is a reciprocal duty on the part of the hearer. He should come with a purpose, and he should come with a prayer. He should come hopeful of benefit, and bestirring all his faculties, that he may miss nothing which is "profitable for doctrine, for reproof, for instruction in righteousness." He should come with a benevolent prepossession towards his pastor, and with a friendly solicitude for his fellow-hearers. And thus, as iron sharpens iron, so his intelligent countenance would animate the speaker; and, like a Hur or an Aaron, his silent petitions would contribute to the success of the sermon.

Nor can aught be more fatal than a habit of indolent hearing. Like one who glances into a mirror, and sees disorder in his attire, or dust on his face, and says, "I must attend to this," but forthwith forgets it, and hurries out on his journey; or who, in the time of plague, sees the livid marks on his countenance, and says, "I must take advice for this," and thinks no more about it till he drops death-stricken on the pavement: so there are languid or luxurious listeners to the Word of God. At the moment, they say, Very true, or, Very good, and they resolve to take some action; but just as the mirror is not medicine,—as even a watery mirror cannot wash from the countenance the specks which it reveals, if merely looked into, —so a self-survey in the clearest sermon will neither erase the blemishes from your character, nor expel the sin-plague from your soul. "Wherefore, my beloved brethren, let every man be swift to hear. And, laying apart all filthiness and superfluity of naughtiness, receive with meekness the engrafted word, which is able to save your souls. But be ye doers of the word, and not hearers only, deceiving your own selves. For if any be a hearer of the word and not a doer, he is like unto a man beholding his natural face in a glass: for he beholdeth himself, and goeth his way, and straightway forgetteth what manner of man he was. But whoso looketh into the perfect law of liberty, and continueth therein,"—like a man who seeing his bedusted visage in the mirror of that polished flood, loses not a moment but makes a laver of his looking-glass, —"he being not a forgetful hearer, but a doer of the work, this man shall be blessed in his deed:"* he shall be saved by his promptitude; or, if saved already, he shall become a more beautiful character by his strenuous self-application.

2. In devotional exercises be intent and deliberate, vers. 2, 3. Like a dream which is a medley from the waking day,—which into its own warp of delirium weaves a shred from all the day's engagements: so, could a fool's prayer be exactly reproduced, it would be a tissue of trifles intermingled with vain repetitions. In all the multitude of words it might be found that there was not a single sincere confession, not one heart-felt and heaven-arresting supplication.

For such vain repetitions the remedy still is reverence. "Be not rash," but remember at whose throne you are kneeling; and be not verbose, but let your words be few and em-

* James i. 19–25.

phatic, as of one who is favored with an audience from Heaven's King. It is right to have stated seasons of worship; but it were also well if with our acts of devotion we could combine some special errand; and it might go far to give precision and urgency to our morning or evening prayer, if for a few moments beforehand we considered whether there were any sin to confess, any duty or difficulty demanding special grace, any friend or any object for which we ought to intercede. And when the emergencies of life—some perplexity or sorrow, some deliverance or mercy, at an unwonted season sends us to the Lord, without any lengthened preamble we should give to this originating occasion the fulness of our feelings and the foremost place in our petitions.

3. In like manner, be not rash with vows and religious promises, verses 4–7. In the old Levitical economy there was large provision made for spontaneous vows and votive offerings; and in our own Christian time there are occasions for vows virtual or implied. It is a vow or a solemn promise which a pastor

makes when he assumes an office in the Christian Church; and it is a virtual vow which every disciple makes when he becomes a member of that Church: equivalent to the oath of fidelity which a citizen takes when he becomes a soldier, or a servant of the Crown. And occasionally, for the carrying out of some great enterprise, it may be expedient that like-minded men should join together, and covenant to stand by one another till the reform or the philanthropic object is effected. But if Christians make voluntary vows at all, it should be with clear warrant from the Word, for purposes obviously attainable, and for limited periods of time. The man who vows to offer a certain prayer at a given hour for all his remaining life, may find it perfectly convenient for the next six months, but not for the next six years. The man who vows to pious uses half the income of the year may be safe; whereas the Jephthah who rashly devotes contingencies over which he has no control may pierce himself through with many sorrows. And whilst every believer feels it his reasonable service to present himself to God a living sacrifice, those who wish to walk in the liberty of sonship will seek to make their dedication, as a child is devoted to its parents, not so much in the stringent precision of a legal document, as in the daily forthgoings of a filial mind.

The glory of Gospel worship consists in its freedom, its simplicity, and its spirituality. We have boldness to enter into the holiest, by the blood of Jesus; and we are encouraged to draw near with a true heart in full assurance of faith. We are not come to a burning mount, nor to the sound of a trumpet and a voice of terror; but we are come "to Jesus, the Mediator of the new covenant, and to the blood of sprinkling, that speaketh better things than that of Abel." The Father seeks true worshippers, such as will worship Him in spirit and in truth; and now that sacrifice and offering have ceased,—and now that burdensome observances have vanished away, praise and prayer and almsgiving are the ordinary oblations of the Christian Church. But surely the freedom of our worship should not abate from its fervor; and because it is simple, there is the more scope for sincerity, and the more need that it should be the worship of the heart and soul. But do we sufficiently realize our privileged but solemn position as worshippers of Him, to whom Seraphim continually do cry, "Holy, holy, holy is the Lord of hosts; the whole earth is full of his glory?" Do we sufficiently realize our blessedness as fellow-worshippers with those who sing on high, "Worthy is the Lamb that was slain?" In the house of prayer, do we make worship our study, and devotion our business? Do we "labor mightily in prayer," and do we "wake up our glory to sing and give praise?" Or are not many of us content to be lookers-on at the prayers, and listeners to the psalmody? and instead of "a golden vial full of odors," is not many a devotional act a vain oblation, a vapid form; a tedium to ourselves and an offence to the Most High?

Beloved, let us bestir ourselves in worship. Let us "make a joyful noise unto the Lord;"

let us "serve him with gladness." Let us sing his praises "with grave and sweet melody," and "with grace in our hearts." And let us concentrate our thoughts, and join zealously in the confessions, the thanksgivings, and the supplications of the public prayers. And thus, like the restful activity of the temple above, we shall find moments pass swiftly which may now be a weariness; and refreshed by the sacred exertion which enlisted our faculties, and which enlivened our feelings, we shall retire sweetly conscious that it was "good to be there."

Finally, my friends, amidst the assurance and gladness of Gospel worship, let us take care that we lose nothing of our veneration and godly fear. "God is greatly to be feared in the assembly of the saints, and to be had in reverence of all them that are about Him." "Thou hast a mighty arm; strong is Thy hand, and high is Thy right hand. Justice and judgment are the habitation of Thy throne; mercy and truth shall go before Thy face." It is a poor religion in which reverence is not a conspicuous element; and, like Moses in the mount, if a man has really communed with God, there will be something awful in the shining of his face. And just as in a far inferior matter,—our relations to one another,—just as you never respect the man who does not respect the noble spirits and exalted intellects among his fellows; whilst you always feel that wherever there is admiration of the great and good there is the germ of principle, the possibility of eminent excellence:—so be it the homely peasant or the village patriarch; be it the philosopher* always pausing before he uttered the Name Supreme, or Israel's destined lawgiver, putting his shoes from off his feet on Horeb's holy ground;—you always feel that to realize heaven's majesty is itself majestic, and that there is nothing in itself more venerable than habitual veneration.

* Boyle

LECTURE XI

The Exchange.

READ ECCLES. v. 9–20; vi. 1–9.

"He that loveth silver shall not be satisfied with silver.

THIS passage describes the vanity of riches. With the enjoyments of frugal industry it contrasts the woes of wealth. Looking up from that condition on which Solomon looked down, it may help to reconcile us to our lot, if we remember how the most opulent of princes envied it.

1. In all grades of society human subsistence is very much the same. "The profit of the earth is for all; the king himself is served by the field." "What hath the wise more than the fool?" Even princes are not fed with ambrosia, nor do poets subsist on asphodel.

Bread and water, the produce of the flocks and the herds, and a few homely vegetables, form the staple of his food who can lay the globe under tribute; and these essentials of healthful existence are within the attainment of ordinary industry. "The profit of the earth is for all."

2. When a man begins to amass money, he begins to feed an appetite which nothing can appease, and which its proper food will only render fiercer. "He that loveth silver shall not be satisfied with silver." To greed there may be "increase," but no increase can ever be "abundance." For, could you change all the pebbles on the beach into minted money, or conjure into bank-notes all the leaves of the forest; nay, could you transmute the solid earth into a single lump of gold, and drop it into the gaping mouth of avarice, it would only be a crumb of transient comfort, a cordial drop enabling it to cry a little louder, Give, give. Therefore happy they who have never got enough to awaken the accumulating passion, and who, feeling that food and raiment are the

utmost to which they can aspire, are therewith content.

3. It is another consideration which should reconcile us to the want of wealth: that, as abundance grows, so grow the consumers, and of riches less perishable, the proprietor enjoys no more than the mere spectator. "When goods increase, they are increased that eat them; and what good is there to the owners thereof, saving the beholding of them with their eyes?" It is so far well that rank in volves a retinue, and that no man can be so selfishly sumptuous but that his luxury gives employment and subsistence to others. On the other hand, it is also well that riches cannot retain in exclusive monopoly the pleasures they procure. A rich man buys a picture or a statue, and he is proud to think that his mansion is adorned with such a famous masterpiece. But a poor man comes and looks at it, and, because he has the æsthetic insight, in a few minutes he is conscious of more astonishment and pleasure than the dull proprietor has experienced in half a century. Or, a rich man

lays out a park or a garden, and, except the diversion of planning and remodelling, he has derived from it little enjoyment; but some bright morning a holiday student or a town-pent tourist comes, and when he leaves he carries with him a freight of life-long recollections. The porter at the gates should have orders to intercept such appropriating sight-seers; for, though they leave the canvass on the walls, and the marble in the gallery,—though they leave the flowers in the vases, and the trees in the forest, they have carried off the glory and the gladness; their bibulous eyes have drunk a delectation, and all their senses have absorbed a joy for which the owner vainly pays his heavy yearly ransom.

4. Amongst the pleasures of obscurity, or rather of occupation, the next noticed is sound slumber. "The sleep of a laboring man is sweet, whether he eat little or much; but the abundance of the rich will not suffer him to sleep." Sometimes the wealthy would be the better for a taste of poverty; it would reveal to them their privileges. But if the poor could

get a taste of opulence, it would reveal to them strange luxuries in lowliness. Fevered with late hours and false excitement, or scared by visions the righteous recompense of gluttonous excess, or with breath suppressed and palpitating heart listing the fancied footsteps of the robber, grandeur often pays a nightly penance for the triumph of the day. As a king expresses it, who could sympathize with Solomon:—

"How many thousands of my poorest subjects
Are at this hour asleep!—Sleep, gentle sleep!
Nature's soft nurse, how have I frighted thee,
That thou no more wilt weigh my eyelids down,
And steep my senses in forgetfulness!
Why rather, sleep, liest thou in smoky cribs,
Upon uneasy pallets stretching thee,
And hushed with buzzing night-flies to thy slumber,
Than in the perfumed chambers of the great,
Under the canopies of costly state,
And lull'd with sounds of sweetest melody?
Then, happy, lowly clown!
Uneasy lies the head that wears a crown."*

5. Wealth is often the ruin of its possessor. It is "kept for the owner to his hurt." Like that King of Cyprus who made himself so rich

* Henry IV., Second Part.

that he became a tempting spoil, and who, rather than lose his treasures, embarked them in perforated ships; but, wanting courage to draw the plugs, ventured back to land and lost both his money and his life:* so a fortune is a great perplexity to its owner, and is no defence in times of danger. And very often, by enabling him to procure all that heart can wish, it pierces him through with many sorrows. Ministering to the lust of the eye, the lust of the flesh, and the pride of life, misdirected opulence has ruined many both in soul and body.

6. Nor is it a small vexation to have accumulated a fortune, and when expecting to transmit it to some favorite child, to find it suddenly swept away. (Vers. 14–16.) There is now the son, but where is the sumptuous mansion? Here is the heir, but where is the vaunted heritage?

7. Last of all, are the infirmity and fretfulness which are the frequent companions of

* Procul dubio hic non possedit divitias, sed a divitiis possessus est; titulo rex insulæ, animo pecuniæ miserabile mancipium.—*Valerius Maximus*, lib. ix. cap. 4.

wealth. "All his days also he eats in darkness, and suffers anxiety and peevishness along with sickness." You pass a stately mansion, and as the powdered menials are closing the shutters of the brilliant room, and you see the sumptuous table spread and the fire-light flashing on vessels of gold and vessels of silver, perhaps no pang of envy pricks your bosom, but a glow of gratulation for a moment fills it; Happy people who tread carpets so soft, and who swim through halls so splendid! But, some future day, when the candles are lighted and the curtains drawn in that self-same apartment, it is your lot to be within; and as the invalid owner is wheeled to his place at the table, and as dainties are handed round of which he dares not taste, and as the guests interchange cold courtesy, and all is so stiff and so common-place, and so heartlessly grand,—your fancy cannot help flying off to some humbler spot with which you are more familiar, and "where quiet with contentment makes her home." Nay, how curious the contrast, could the thoughts be read which sometimes cross one another! That ragged urchin who opened the common-gate, and let the silvery chariot through,—oh, "what a phantom of delight" the lady looked as in clouds of cushions and on a firmament of ultramarine she floated away! What a golden house she must have come from, and what a happy thing to be borne about from place to place in such a carriage, as easy as a bird and as brilliant as a queen! But, little boy, that lady looked at you. As she passed she noticed your ruddy cheeks, and she envied you. That glittering chariot was carrying what you do not know—a broken heart; and death-stricken and world-weary, as she looked at you, she thought, How pleasant to have lived amongst the blossomed May-trees on this common's edge, and never known the falsehoods of fashion and the evil ways of the world!

We have glanced at the sorrows of the rich; some will expect that we should now descant on the sinfulness of riches. And a certain class of religionists, misunderstanding the Saviour's precept, "Lay not up for yourselves treasures on earth," have spoken of money as if it were a malignant principle, and have canonized poverty as a Christian grace. Fully carried out, this theory would prohibit the flagon of oil and the barrel of meal, and would reduce us all to the widow's cruse and handful; for it makes little difference whether the hoard be in kind, or packed up in the portable form of money. It would justify the life of the anchorite who has no funded property except the roots in the ground and the nuts on the trees; and it would suit very well such a state of society as Israel spent in the desert, when no skill could secure a week's manna beforehand, and when the same pair of shoes lasted forty years. But as it was not for a world of anchorites or ascetics,—as it was not for a society on which the clouds should rain miraculous supplies that the Saviour was legislating,—his words must have another meaning. And what is that? Live by faith. Look forward: look upward. Let nothing temporal be your treasure. Whether your abode be a hut or a castle, think only of the Father's house as your enduring mansion. Whether your friends be high or low, coarse or refined, think only of just men made perfect as your permanent associates. And whether your possessions be great or small, think only of the joys at God's right hand as your eternal treasure. Lead a life disentangled and expedite—setting your affections on things above, and never so clinging to the things temporal as to lose the things eternal.

Translated into its equivalent, money just means food and clothing, and a salubrious dwelling. It means instructive books, and rational recreation. It means freedom from anxiety, and leisure for personal improvement. It means the education of one's children, and the power of doing good to others. And to inveigh against it, as if it were intrinsically sinful, is as fanatical as it would be to inveigh against the bread and the raiment, the books and the Bibles, which the money procures. It would be to stultify all those precepts which tell us to provide things honest in the sight of all men; to do good and to communicate; to help forward destitute saints after a godly sort; to make friends of the unrighteous mammon.

And as there is nothing in the Bible to prohibit the acquirement of wealth, there is much to guide us in its right bestowment. Using but not abusing God's bounties, the Christian avoids both the wasteful and the penurious extremes, and is neither a miser nor a spendthrift. With that most elastic and enlightened disciple, who knew so well how to be abased and how to abound, the believer can say, "I have learned in whatsoever state I am, therewith to be content. Everywhere and in all things, I am instructed, both to be full and to be hungry, both to abound and suffer need. I can do all things through Christ who strengtheneth me."

It was a sultry day, and an avaricious old man who had hoarded a large amount, was toiling away and wasting his little remaining strength, when a heavenly apparition stood before him. "I am Solomon," it said, with a friendly voice; "what are you doing?" "If you are Solomon," answered the old man, "how can you ask? When I was young you sent me to the ant, and told me to consider her ways; and from her I learned to be industrious and gather stores." "You have only half-learned your lesson," replied the spirit; "go once more to the ant, and learn to rest the winter of your years and enjoy your collected treaures."* And this lesson of moderate but cheerful spending, nothing teaches so effectually as the gospel. Reminding the believer that the life is more than meat, and the body more than raiment, it also suggests to him that meat and raiment are more than money; and by saving him from the idolatry of wealth, it emboldens him to use it: so that far from feeling impoverished when it is converted into some worthy equivalent, he can use with thankfulness the gifts which his Heavenly Father sends him. Within the bounds of temperance and forethought, he subscribes to the sentiment of our text, "It is good and comely to eat and to drink, and to enjoy the good of one's labor; for the power to eat thereof and to take his portion is itself the gift of God."

* Lessing's Fables.

But Christianity teaches a lesson higher still. "Remembering the words of our Lord Jesus. how he said, It is more blessed to give than to receive," the true disciple will value wealth chiefly as he can spend it on objects dear to his dear Lord. To him money is a talent and a trust; and he will feel it a fine thing to have a fortune, because it enables him to do something notable for some noble end. And whether, like Granville Sharpe, he spends it in pleading the cause of the oppressed and the friendless: or, like Howard, devotes it to reclaim the most depraved and degraded; or, like Simeon, purchases advowsons in order to appoint faithful pastors; or, like Thomas Wilson, multiplies places of worship in a crowded metropolis; there is no fortune which brings to its possessor such a return of solid satisfaction as that which is converted into Christian philanthropy. Our houses tumble down; our monuments decay; our equipages grow frail and shabby. But it is a fine thing to have a fortune, and so be able to give a grand impulse to some important cause. It is a happy thing to have wealth enough to set fairly afloat an emancipation movement or a prison reform. It is a noble thing to be rich enough to provide Gospel ordinances for ten thousand people in a vast and world-wielding capital. It is a blessed thing to be "a man to whom God has not only given riches and wealth," but so large a heart,—so beneficent, so brotherly, that his fruition of his fortune is as wide as the thousands who share it, and the reversion as secure as the heaven in which it is treasured.

LECTURE XII.

Borrowed Lights for a Dark Landing-place.

"That which hath been is named already, and it is known what man is: neither may he contend with him that is mightier than he. Seeing there be many things that increase vanity what is man the better? For who knoweth what is good for man in this life, all the days of his vain life which he spendeth as a shadow? for who can tell a man what shall be after him under the sun?"—ECCLES. VI. 10–12.

YOU have ascended a staircase which, inside the solid rock, wound up from the sands of the sea-shore to green fields and beautiful gardens. Somewhat of this sort is the structure of Ecclesiastes. And now we have reached the half-way landing-place, the dimmest and coldest station in the entire ascent; and very mournful is the strain in which our moralist reviews his progress. "Fate is fixed, and man is feeble; joy is but a phantom, and life a vapor, and darkness veils the future." Truly, we have need to borrow lamps and suspend them in this dark place. We must send for some brighter minstrel; for our hearts will break if we only listen to the bard of vanity.

I. Fate is fixed. "That which hath been or which is to be, hath been named already; neither may man contend with him that is mightier than he." All the past was the result of a previous destiny, and so shall be all the future. Everything is fate. Such is the sentiment of the third chapter, and such appears to be the import of this passage. "Since fate bears sway, and everything must be as it is, why dost thou strive against it?"*

Brethren, is there never such a feeling in your minds? Do you never feel as if you were the subjects of a stern ordination? Do you never say, "I must obey my destiny? It is of no use contending with fate. Mine is an unlucky star, and I can change neither my nature nor my nativity; so I must abide my time and take my doom." Do you never feel

* Marcus Antoninus xii. 13.

as if you were driven along a path over which you have no control, and as if the power propelling you were a blind and inexorable necessity?

Partly imbibed from the old classics, and partly from a sound theology sullenly spoken; and partly indigenous to the human heart, which, even when it does not believe in God and in Jesus, cannot believe in chance, the feeling now expressed is far from rare; and just as it seems to have visited Solomon in the thoughtful interludes of his vanity, so the more pensive and musing spirits are likely to feel it most. As it contains a certain admixture of truth, on a principle which we have frequently adopted in these lectures, we shall go to a greater than Solomon in order to get that partial truth corrected and completed.

In the outset, it must be conceded that the Saviour assumed a pre-ordination in all events. He was constantly using such language as this: "The hour is come;" "The hairs of your head are all numbered;" "Your names are written in heaven;" "Many be called, but few chosen;" "No man can come to me, except the Father draw him;" "For the elect's sake, whom he hath chosen, God hath shortened the days;" "To my sheep I give eternal life." But then, what sort of pre-ordination was it which the Saviour recognized? Was it mechanical, or moral? Was it blind destiny, or a wise decree? Was it the evolution of a dark necessity, or "the determinate counsel and foreknowledge of God?" Was it the fiat of an abstract law, or the will of a living Person? In one word, was it FATE, or was it PROVIDENCE?

Most comforting is it to study this doctrine with the great Prophet for our tutor, and so to see the propitious aspect which it bears when rightly understood. As interpreted by "the only-begotten Son from the bosom of the Father," that pre-arrangement of events which the theologian calls predestination, and which the philosopher calls necessity, and which old heathenism called fate, is nothing more than the will of the Father,—the good pleasure of that blessed and only Potentate whose omniscience foresaw all possibilities, and from out of all these possibilities whose benevolent wisdom selected the best and gave it being. And he alone can understand election, or exult in Providence, who in right of the Surety can look up to God as his Father, and so take the same views of the Father's purposes as the Saviour took, equally revering the majestic fixity of the firm decree, equally rejoicing in its wise foresight and paternal kindness. "Fear not, little flock; it is *your Father's* GOOD PLEASURE to give you the kingdom." "I thank Thee, *O Father*, Lord of heaven and earth, because thou hast hid these things from the wise and prudent, and hast revealed them unto babes. Even so, Father, for so it seemed *good in thy sight.*" "*The hour is come*, that the Son of man should be glorified. *Father*, glorify thy name." And just as you might imagine some poor wandered child waking up amidst the din and tumult of a factory, and cowering half-delinquent, half-stupified, into his dusky corner,—afraid lest this thunderous enginery rush in on him and rend him to pieces, and still more paralyzed when he perceives in its movements the indications of an awful order, —the whole spinning and whirling, clashing aud clanking, in obedience to a mysterious and invisible power. But whilst he is watching from his hiding-place, another child comes in, of an age about his own; and this other walks fearlessly forward, for his father leads him by the hand, and shows him the beautiful fabrics which are flowing forth from all the noisy mechanism; or if there be some point in their progress where there is risk to his child from the flashing wheels, he speaks a word and that portion stands still; for his father is owner of it all. So to the poor waif of mortality, the outcast child of apostate Adam,—to the godlesss pirit waking up in this world of rapid revolution and tumultuous resonance, there is an awful aspect of fatality on the one side and a crushing sense of impotence on the other. So selfish is man and so cruel is the world; so strange are life's reverses, and so irresistible is the progress of events, that he momentarily expects to be annihilated by the strong and remorseless mechanism;—when, in the midst of all the turmoil he perceives one of like passions with himself walking calmly up and down, and fearing no evil, for his Father is with him, and that Father is contriver and controller of the whole. So, my friends, it depends on our point of view whether the fixed succession of events shall appear as a sublime arrangement or a dire necessity. It depends on whether we recognize ourselves as foundlings in the universe, or the children of God by faith in Jesus Christ,—it depends on this, whether in the mighty maze we discern the decrees of fate, or the presiding wisdom of our heavenly Father. It depends on whether we are still skulking in the obscure corner, aliens, intruders, outlaws; or walking at liberty, with filial spirit and filial security,—whether we shall be more panic-stricken by the power of the mechanism, or more enchanted with its beautiful products. It depends on whether we are spectators or sons, whether our emotion towards the Divine foreknowledge and sovereignty be, "O fate, I fear thee," or, "O Father, I thank thee."

II. Man is feeble. "It is known what man is; neither may he contend with him that is mightier than he." And Christless humanity is a very feeble thing. His bodily frame is feeble. A punctured nerve or a particle of sand will sometimes occasion it exquisite anguish; a grape-seed or an insect's sting has been known to consign it to dissolution. And man's intellect is feeble; or, rather, it is a strange mixture of strength and weakness:—

"Go, wondrous creature! mount where science guides;
Go, measure earth, weigh air, and state the tides;
Instruct the planets in what orbs to run,
Correct old Time, and regulate the sun;
Go, soar with Plato to the empyreal sphere,
To the first good, first perfect, and first fair;
Go, teach Eternal Wisdom how to rule—
Then drop into thyself, and be a fool!"*

Nevertheless, redeemed and regenerate humanity is only a little lower than the angels. Its materialism was worn by the Son of God Incarnate, and as He wore it, it was found a

* Pope's "Essay on Man," Ep. ii.

shrine in which perfect goodness could exist, and one from which not a few of its endearing rays could emanate; and, celestialized, that corporeity will find a place in the new heavens and new earth where righteousness dwelleth. And, sublime and sanctified, man's intellect is fit for the noblest themes in the loftiest society. Not to speak of Moses' meek sagacity, and David's lyric raptures, and Solomon's startling intuitions; there are sons of Adam who, here, on earth, possessed no knowledge beyond simple apprehension or idiot ignorance, and who are now the immediate pupils of the Bright and Morning Star, and fellow-students with the seraphim. And though it be madness in man to contend with his Maker, it is man's prerogative that his very weakness is a purchase on Omnipotence. Insane when contending with One that is mightier, he is irresistible when in faith and coincidence of holy affection he fights the battles of the Most High, and when by prayer and uplooking affiance, he imports into his own imbecility the might of Jehovah. It is known what man is, and what mere man can do. A Samson can rend the ravening lion, and return to find his bleached ribs a hive of honey. A Goliath can hold at bay the embattled host, and with his beam-like lance beat back a charging company. David's three champions can hew their way through the host of the Philistines, and from the well of Bethlehem bear triumphant to the camp their costly flask of water. And thus, the potsherds of the earth can strive with the potsherds of the earth, and a strong one destroy the weaker. But it is hardly known yet what man can do when his Maker contends for him and fights through him; although the temptations which Joseph and Daniel have vanquished, and found their demolished strength replaced by sweetness; the terror of God which a solitary Elijah or John Baptist has stricken into an idolatrous or hypocritical generation; the water of life which Paul and Silas and Timothy have carried into the midst of a dying world through pain and peril, through bitter mockings and daily deaths,—although these moral triumphs and religious trophies are earnests and examples of what may be done by man when, through Christ strengthening, man is rendered superhuman.

III. Every joy is futile. It is only fresh food for the life-wasting vanity; more fat kine for the lean ones to devour and convert into tenuity; more must poured into the working vat in order to acidify and augment the brewage of vexation. "Seeing there be many things that increase vanity, what is man the better?" What the better is man of that reputation which only makes him more envied? What the better is he of that wealth which only makes him more obnoxious to plots and dangers? What the better of that philosophy which, like a taper on the face of a midnight cliff, only shows how beetling is the brow above him, and how profound the gulf below, whilst he himself is crawling a wingless reptile on the ever-narrowing ledge? What the better is acquirement, when, after all, man's intellect, man's conscience, man's affections must remain a vast and unappeasable vacuity?

Here it is that the other Royal Preacher

comes forward, and, instead of echoing, answers the demand of Solomon. Jesus says, "I am the bread of life: he that cometh to me shall never hunger, and he that believeth on me shall never thirst." Jesus is God manifest, and, therefore, Jesus known is satisfaction to the famished intellect. He is God reconciled, and, therefore, Jesus trusted is comfort to the aching conscience. He is God communicated, and, therefore, Jesus loved is a continual feast to the hungry affections. Incarnate, atoning, interceding, Immanuel is the bread of life,—the only sustenance and satisfaction of the immortal soul. And, O my hearers, if any of you are hungry, make trial of this food. If your conscience hungers, feed on some faithful saying till you find it as sweet as it is solid, as refreshing as 'tis true. "God loved the world and gave his Son." "Christ Jesus came into the world to save sinners." "His blood cleanseth from all sin." "Him that cometh unto me, I will in no wise cast out." "Behold the Lamb of God!" Dwell on such sayings till they have sunk into your spirit's core and spread through your consenting nature in realizations glad and blissful. Does your understanding hunger? Do you pine for some knowledge absolute, conclusive, positive? Then no man knoweth the Father save the Son, and he to whom the Son shall reveal him. Look to Jesus. Study the Word made flesh. In Him dwells all the fulness of the Godhead bodily. In Him, the express image of the Father, behold at once your Teacher and your task; for Jesus is the true Theology. Sit at the Saviour's feet, and listen to his words; for God is all which Jesus says. Look into his countenance, for God is all which Jesus is. And do your affections hunger? From the festivals of earth,—from its feasts of friendship even, do you sometimes retire mortified and almost misanthropic? or, like the reveller glancing up at the thread-suspended sword, or gazing at the fulgorous finger as it flames along the wall, have you misgivings in the unhallowed mercies which you enjoy aloof from God, or in the place of God, or beneath the wrath of God? Then, through the Mediator be reconciled to God. In Christ accept Him as your Friend and Father. Enter into his peace, and learn to delight in his perfections; and thus, whilst sinful pleasures lose their relish, lawful joys will acquire a flavor of sacredness, and the zest is a sweet security. Or should the cistern break and the creature fail, the infinite joy is Jehovah, and the soul cannot wither whose roots are replenished from that fountain unfailing.

IV. Life is fleeting. It is a "vain life," and all its days a "shadow." A shadow is the nearest thing to a nullity. It is seldom noticed. Even "a vapor" in the firmament,—a cloud may catch the eye, and in watching its changing hues or figure you may find the amusement of a moment; and if that cloud condense into a shower, a few fields may thank it for its timely refreshment. But a shadow,—the shadow of a vapor! who notes it? who records it? As it sails along the mountain side, with morning bright behind it, and summer noon before it, the daisy does not care to wink, nor does the hare-bell droop, nor does the bee suspend its labors; and at eve, the shepherd-boy cross-questioned cannot tell if any cloud there were. And the case is rare where some panting traveller sighs, "Return, O shadow! Kind vapor, I wish you would not vanish!"

But Jesus Christ hath brought immortality to light. This fleeting life He has rendered important as "a shadow from the rock eternity." "I am the Resurrection and the Life: whosoever liveth and believeth in me shall never die." In his own teaching, and in the teaching of his apostles, the present existence acquires a fearful consequence as the germ, or rather as the outset of one which is never-ending. To their view, this existence is both everything and nothing. As the commencement of eternity, and as giving its complexion to all the changeless future, it is everything; as the competitor of that eternity or the counterpoise to its joys and sorrows it is nothing. "What shall it profit a man, if he shall gain the whole world, and lose his own soul?" "Fear not them who kill the body, but are not able to kill the soul: but rather fear Him who is able to destroy both soul and body in hell." "Our light affliction, which is but for a moment, worketh for us a far more exceeding and eternal weight of glory; while we look not at the things which are seen, but at the things which are not seen: for the things which are seen are temporal; but the things which are not seen are eternal." "How vain, then, are men, who, seeing life so short, endeavor to live long and not to live well!"* How vain are men who, pronouncing the present life a shadow, neglect to secure the everlasting substance!

V. The future is a dark enigma. "Who can tell a man what shall be after him under the sun?"

Says Dr. Stewart of Moulin, "I remember an old, pious, very recluse minister, whom I used to meet once a-year. He scarcely ever looked at a newspaper. When others were talking about the French Revolution, he showed no concern or curiosity about it. He

* Jeremy Taylor's "Works," vol. iii. p. 418.

said he knew from the Bible how it would all end, better than the most sagacious politician, —that the Lord reigns,—that the earth will be filled with his glory,—that the Gospel will be preached to all nations,—and that all subordinate events are working out these great ends. This was enough for him, and he gave himself no concern about the news or events of the day, only saying, It shall be well with the righteous."* And although no man can tell the conqueror how it shall be with the dynasty he has founded; nor the poet how it shall be with the epic he has published; nor the capitalist how it shall be with the fortune he has accumulated; it is easy to tell the philanthropist and the Christian how it shall be, not only with himself, but with the cause he is so eagerly promoting. And without quenching curiosity, it may quiet all anxiety to know that when he himself is gone to be forever with the Lord, Christ's kingdom will be spreading in the world. "Then said I, O my Lord, what shall be the end of these things?

* Memoirs of Dr. Stewart, p. 336.

And he said, Go thy way, Daniel; for the words are closed up and sealed. Go thou thy way till the end be, for thou shalt rest, and stand in thy lot at the end of the days."

LECTURE XIII.

A Good Name.

"A good name is better than precious ointment."—
ECCLES. VII. 1.

AT this point we come out into a purer-atmosphere; we emerge upon a higher platform; and, if we have not day-spring, we have the harbingers of dawn.

Hitherto the book has chiefly contained the diagnosis of the great disease. Repeating the successive symptoms as they developed in himself, the Royal patient has passed before us in every variety of mood, from the sleepy collapse of one who has eaten the fabled lotus, up to the frantic consciousness of a Hercules tearing his limbs as he tries to rend off his robe of fiery poison. He now comes to the cure. He enumerates the prescriptions which he tried, and mentions their results. Most of them afforded some relief. They made him "better." But they were only palliatives. There was something which always impaired their efficacy; and it is only at the very end that he announces the great panacea, and gives us what is better than a thousand palliatives,—an unfailing specific.

The recipes contained in this and the subsequent chapters availed to mitigate Solomon's vexation, but they failed to cure it. They mitigated it, because each of them was one ingredient of the great specific; they failed to cure it, because they were only isolated ingredients. Each maxim of virtue is conducive to happy living; but the love of God is the vitality of all virtue; and, in order to secure its full practical value, we must supply to each separate maxim the great animating motive. A rule of conduct which is "dead, so long as it abideth alone," may be very helpful when quickened, and when occupying its appropriate place in a system of evangelical ethics.

Solomon's first beatitude is an honorable reputation. He knew what it had been to possess it; and he knew what it was to lose it. And here he says, Happy is the possessor of an untarnished character! so happy that he cannot die too soon! "A good name is better than precious ointment; and (to its owner) the day of death is better than the day of birth."

A name truly good is the aroma from virtuous character. It is a spontaneous emanation from genuine excellence. It is a reputation for whatsoever things are honest and lovely, and of good report. It is such a name as is not only remembered on earth but written in heaven. The names of Abel and Enoch and Noah are good names, and so are all which have been transmitted in that "little book of martyrs," the eleventh of Hebrews: those "elders" who not only obtained the Church's good report, through faith, but who had this testimony, "that they pleased God." But in order to a good name something else is needed besides a good nature. Flowers have bloomed in the desert which were only viewed by God and the angels; and there have been solitary saints whose holiness was only recognized by Him who created it, and by just men made perfect. And so wicked is this world that much excellence may have vanished from its surface unknown and unsuspected. The Inquisition has, no doubt, extinguished many an Antipas, and in the Sodoms of our earth many a Lot has vexed his soul and died with no Pentateuch to preserve his memory. To secure a reputation there must not only be the genuine excellence but the genial atmosphere. There must be some good men to observe and appreciate the goodness while it lived, and others to foster its memory when gone. But should both combine,—the worth and the appreciation of worth,—the resulting good name is better than precious ointment. Rarer and more costly, it is also one of the most salutary influences that can penetrate society. For, just as a box of spikenard is not only valuable to its possessor, but pre-eminently precious in its diffusion; so, when a name is really good, it is of unspeakable service to all who are capable of feeling its exquisite inspiration.

And should the Spirit of God so replenish a man with his gifts and graces, as to render his name thus wholesome, better than the day of his birth will be the day of his death; for at death the box is broken and the sweet savor spreads abroad. There is an end of the envy and sectarianism and jealousy, the detraction and the calumny, which often environ goodness when living; and now that the stopper of prejudice is removed, the world fills with the odor of the ointment, and thousands grow stronger and more lifesome for the good name of one. Better in this respect, better than their birth-day was the dying day of Henry Martyn and Robert M'Cheyne; for the secret of their hidden life was then revealed, and, mingled as it is with the name of Jesus, the Church will never lose the perfume. And in this respect better than their birthday was the dying-day of Dr. Arnold and Sir Fowell Buxton; for men could then forget the offence of controversy and the irritation of party politics, and could surrender to the undiluted charm of healthy piety and heroic Christianity. And better, thus regarded, was the dying-day of Stephen and James and Paul; for every disciple could then forget the infirmities by which some had been annoyed and the faithfulness by which others had been offended, and could treasure up that best of a good man's relics, the memory of a devoted life,—the sweet odour of an unquestioned sanctity.

Do not despise a good name. There is no better heritage that a father can bequeath to his children, and there are few influences on society more wholesome than the fame of its worthies. The names of Luther and Knox, of Hampden and Washington, of Schwartz and Eliot, are still doing good in the world. Nor is there in a family any richer heir-loom than the memory of a noble ancestor. Without a good name you can possess little ascendency over others; and when it has not pioneered your way and won a prepossession for yourself, your patriotic or benevolent intentions are almost sure to be defeated.

And yet it will never do to seek a good name as a primary object. Like trying to be graceful, the effort to be popular will make you contemptible. Take care of your spirit and conduct, and your reputation will take care of itself. It is by "blamelessness and good behavior," that not only bishops, but individual believers, are to gain "a good report of them who are without." The utmost that you are called to do as the custodier of your own reputation is to remove injurious aspersions. Let not your good be evil spoken of, and follow the highest examples in mild and explicit self-vindication. Still, no reputation can be permanent which does not spring from principle: and he who would maintain a good character should be mainly solicitous to maintain a conscience void of offence towards God and towards men.

Where others are concerned the case is different. To our high-principled and deserving brethren, we owe a frank commendation and a fraternal testimony. "To rejoice in their good name; to cover their infirmities; freely to acknowledge their gifts and graces; readily to receive a good report, and unwillingly to admit an evil report concerning them; to discourage tale-bearers and slanderers,"* are duties which we owe to our neighbors; and good names are not so numerous but that the utmost care should be taken of them. When Dr. M'Crie published the Life of our Reformer, it was very noble in Dugald Stewart to seek out the young author in his humble dwelling and cheer him with his earnest eulogy. And when one of the Reformation heroes was maligned, it was fine to see their advocate rummaging amongst the archives of the Public Library, till the discrepant date enabled him to exclaim, "Thank God! our friend was by that time safe in Abraham's bosom!" It was a happy thing for Paul to have so good a name among the Gentile Churches, that his mere request was enough to bring large contributions to the poor saints of Jerusalem; but, if so, what a happy thought to Barnabas to know that when Paul himself was an object of suspicion to the Church at Jerusalem,† his own good name had been the new convert's passport and guarantee.

* Westminster Larger Catechism † Acts ix. 26, 27.

LECTURE XIV.

The Power of Patience.

"The patient in spirit is better than the proud in spirit."—
ECCLES. VII. 8.

THE lion was caught in the toils of the hunter. The more he tugged, the more his feet got entangled; when a little mouse heard his roaring, and said that if his majesty would not hurt him, he thought he could release him. At first the king of the beasts took no notice of such a contemptible ally; but at last, like other proud spirits in trouble, he allowed his tiny friend to do as he pleased. So one by one, the mouse nibbled through the cords, till he had set free first one foot and then another, and then all the four, and with a growl of hearty gratitude, the king of the forest acknowledged that the patient in spirit is sometimes stronger than the proud in spirit. And it is beautiful to see how, when some sturdy nature is involved in perplexity, and by its violence and vociferation is only wasting its strength without forwarding its escape; there will come in some timely sympathizer, mild and gentle, and will suggest the simple extrication, or by soothing vehemence down into his own tranquillity, will set him on the way to effect his self-deliverance. Even so, all through the range of philanthropy, patience is power. It is not the water-spout, but the nightly dew which freshens vegetation. They are not the flashes of the lightning which mature our harvests, but the daily sunbeams, and that quiet electricity which thrills in atoms and which flushes in every ripening ear. Niagara in all its thunder fetches no fertility; but the Nile, coming without observation, with noiseless fatness overflows, and from under the retiring flood Egypt looks up again, a garner of golden corn. The world is the better for its moral cataracts, and its spiritual thunderbolts; but the influences which do the world's great work,—which freshen and fertilize it, and which are maturing its harvests for the garner of glory, are not the proud and potent spirits, but the patient and the persevering; they are not the noisy and startling phenomena, but the steady and silent operations. They are the Sunday-schools which line upon line repeat the Gospel lesson, and keep alive in our youthful millions some fear of God. They are the good and loving mothers who begin with cradle hymns, and who try to make the sweet story of Jesus as dear and as memorable as their own kind voices. They are the weekly Sabbaths which softly overflow the land, and which, when they ebb again, leave everywhere the freshness and the fertilizing elements conveyed in their heaven-descended tide. Patience is power. In a thirsty land, one farmer digs a pit, and as no water fills it he opens another, and as that also continues, like the well in Dothan, dry, he commences a third in a spot more promising, and a fourth, and many more, till he has tried all his territory without success, and then, chafed and chagrined, he abandons all effort in despair. His neighbor chooses a spot, and begins. No water flows, but he is not discouraged. The spade and the mattock he exchanges for the drill and the auger; and after hammering through the flinty rock for days and weeks, at last the long-sought fountain gushes, and at his threshold he secures a perennial spring, which neither feels the summer drought nor dreads the winter's cold. And so, on behalf of some right object, one man is anxious to enlist the good feeling of humanity: and he brings his project before one influential mind after another, and he is mortified to find how drily it is received by this celebrated philanthropist, and how many difficulties are started by another,—till he is ready to declare that benevolence is all a sham and every patriot a hypocrite. But, strong in faith and patience, another takes the Artesian auger. He knows that deep under our hard humanity there are tender feelings and kind sympathies. Or if it be the Church on which he seeks to operate, he knows that under all its callousness and formalism there circulates a conscience,—there flows a fresh current of principle and love fed from the crystal river, and he is resolved to reach it. He takes the Artesian auger. "One thing I do." Preserving his temper amid all rebuffs, and persevering amidst all impediments, he keeps urging this one object,—and at last the vein is struck —the fountain flows. Charles sees the Bible Society organized, and Carey is sent to India. Raikes sets his Sabbath-schools agoing, and Naismith the City Mission. Sadler sees infant emancipation become a popular movement, and Agnew finds the Church at last aroused to the claims of the Sabbath-day.

LECTURE XV.

Dead Flies.

"Dead flies cause the ointment of the apothecary to send forth a stinking savor: so doth a little folly him that is in reputation for wisdom and honor."—ECCLES. x. 1.

THE people of Palestine dealt largely in aromatic oils, and it was a chief business of their apothecaries to prepare them. A little thing was enough to spoil them. Although the vase were alabaster, and although the most exquisite perfumes were dissolved in the limpid olive, a dead fly could change the whole into a pestilent odor.

And so, says the Royal Moralist, a character may be carefully confected. You may attend to all the rules of wisdom and self-government which I have now laid down; but if you retain a single infirmity it will ruin the whole.

Like the decomposing influence of that dead fly, it will injure all the rest and destroy the reputation which you otherwise merit.

The principle is especially applicable to a Christian profession; and the best use we can make of it is to exemplify it in some of those flaws and failings which destroy the attraction and impressiveness of men truly devout and God-fearing. Our instances must be taken almost at random; for, like their Egyptian prototypes, these flies are too many to be counted.

Rudeness.—Some good men are blunt in their feelings, and rough in their manners; and they apologize for their coarseness by calling it honesty, downrightness, plainness of speech. They quote in self-defence the sharp words, and shaggy mien of Elijah and John the Baptist, and, as affectation, they sneer at the soft address and mild manners of gentler men. Now, it is very true that there is a certain strength of character, an impetuousness of feeling, and a sturdy vehemence of principle, to which it is more difficult to prescribe the rules of Christian courtesy, than to more meek and pliant natures. It is very possible that Latimer in his bluntness, and Knox in his erect and iron severity, and Luther in the magnificent explosions of his far-resounding indignation, may have been nobler natures, and fuller of the grace of God than the supple courtiers whose sensibilities they so rudely shattered. But it does not follow that men who have not got their warfare to wage are entitled to use their weapons. Nor does it even follow that their warfare would have been less successful had they wielded no such weapons. The question, however, is not between two rival graces,—between integrity on the one side, and affability on the other; but the question is, Are these two graces compatible? Can they co-exist? Is it possible for a man to be explicit, and open, and honest, and, withal, courteous and considerate of the feelings of others? Is it possible to add to fervor and fidelity, suavity, and urbanity, and brotherly-kindness? The question has already been answered, for the actual union of these things has already been exhibited. Without referring to Nathan's interview with David, where truth and tenderness triumph together, or Paul's remonstrances to his brethren, in which a melting heart is the vehicle of each needful reproof, we need only revert to the great example itself. In the epistles to the Asiatic Churches, each begins with commendation, wherever there was anything that could be commended. With the magnanimity which remembers past services in the midst of present injury, and which would rather notice good than complain of evil, each message, so far as there was material for it, is ushered in by a word of eulogy, and weight is added to the subsequent admonition by this preface of kindness.* And it was the same while the Lord Jesus was on earth. His tender tone was the keen edge of his reproofs, and his unquestionable love infused solemnity into every warning. There never was one more faithful than the Son of God, but there never was one more considerate. And just as rudeness

* Fuller on the Apocalypse, p. 16.

is not essential to honesty, so neither is rough ness essential to strength of character. The Christian should have a strong character; he should be a man of remarkable decision; he should start back from temptation as from a bursting bomb. And he should be a man of inflexible purpose. When once he knows his Lord's will, he should go through with it, aye, through fire and water with it. But this he may do without renouncing the meekness and gentleness which were in Christ. He may have zeal without pugnacity, determination without obstinacy. He should distinguish between the ferocity of the animal and the courage of the Christian. And whether he makes the distinction or not, the world will make it. The world looks for the serene benevolence of conscious strength in a follower of the Lamb of God; and, however rude its own conduct, it expects that the Christian himself will be courteous.

Irritability.—One of the most obvious and impressive features in the Saviour's character was his meekness. In a patience which ingenious or sudden provocation could not upset; in a magnanimity which insult could not ruffle; in a gentleness from which no folly could extract an unadvised word, men saw what they could scarcely understand, but that which made them marvel. Though disciples were strangely dull, he never lost temper with them; though Judas was very dishonest, He did not bring any railing accusation against him; though Philip had been so long time with Him, and had not understood Him, He did not dismiss him from his company. When Peter denied Him, it was not a frown that withered him, but a glance of affection that melted him. And so with his enemies; it was not by lightning from heaven, but by love from his pierced heart, that He subdued them. But many Christians lack this beauty of their Master's holiness; they are afflicted with evil tempers, they cannot rule their spirits, or rather they do not try. Some indulge occasionally in fits of anger; and others are haunted by habitual, daily, life-long fretfulness. The one sort is generally calm and pellucid as an

Alpine lake, but on some special provocation, is tossed up into a magnificent tempest; the other is like the Bosphorus, in a continual stir, and even when not a breath is moving, by the contrariety of its internal currents vexing itself into a ceaseless whirl and eddy. The one is Hecla—for long intervals silent as a granite peak, and suffering the snow-flakes to fall on its cold crater, till you forget that it is a burning mountain; and then on some sudden and unlooked-for disturbance, hurling the hollow truce into the clouds, and pouring forth in one noisy night the stifled mischief of many a year. The other is Stromboli, a perpetual volcano, seldom indulging in any disastrous eruption; but muttering and quaking, steaming and hissing night and day, in a way which makes strangers nervous; and ever and anon spinning through the air a red-hot rock, or a spirt of molten metal, to remind the heedless natives of their angry neighbor. But either form, the paroxysmal fury, and the perennial fretfulness, is inconsistent with the wisdom from above, which is peaceable, gentle, easy to be entreated. Worldly men can perceive the inconsistency, but instead of ascribing it to its proper causes, they are more likely to attribute it to the insincerity of Christians, or the insufficiency of the Gospel; and even the more willing sort of worldlings, those who have some predisposition in favor of the truth, are very apt to be shocked and driven off by the unhallowed ebullitions of religious men. Suppose such an individual, with his attention newly awakened to the great salvation—with his mind impressed by some Scriptural delineation of regenerate character; his ear, it may be, still charmed with a glowing description of the Gospel's magic power, making wolfish men so lamblike, and teaching the weaned child to play on the cockatrice den; suppose such a man in the way of business, or kindness, or spiritual inquiry, to approach a stranger of Christian renown, and accosting him in full persuasion of his Christian character, prepared for a cordial welcome, a patient hearing at the least,—but alas! coming in at some unpropitious moment, he is greeted with a shout of impatience, or annihilated by a flash from his lowering countenance,—why, it is like putting your hand into the nest of the turtle-dove, and drawing it out with a long, slimy serpent, dangling in warty folds, and holding on by its fiery fangs. There is horror in the disappointment, as well as anguish in the bite; and the frightful association cannot easily be forgotten.

Akin to these infirmities of temper, are some other inconsistencies as inconvenient to their Christian brethren as they are likely to stumble a scoffing world. Some professors are so whimsical and impracticable, that it needs continual stratagem to enlist them in any labor of usefulness, and after they are once fairly engaged in it, nothing but perpetual watchfulness and the most tender management can keep them in it. In all your dealings with them, like a man walking over a galvanic pavement, you tread uneasily, wondering when the next shock is to come off, and every moment expecting some paradox to spring under your feet. In the Christian societies of which they are members, they constitute non-conformable materials of which it is difficult to dispose. They are irregular solids for which it is not easy to find a place in rearing the temple. They are the polyhedrons of the church, each punctilio of their own forming a several face, and making it a hard problem to fix them where they will not mar the structure. Apostolical magnanimity they deem subserviency or sinful connivance; and simultaneous movements or Christian co-operation they deem lawful only when all conform to them. Like those individuals whose bodies are non-conductors, and who can stop an electric circuit after it has travelled through a mile of other men, sectarian professors are so positively charged with their own peculiarities, that the influence which has been transmitted through consenting myriads, stops short as soon as it reaches them.

Selfishness.—The world expects self-denial in the Christian; and with reason, for of all men he can best afford it, and by his profession he is committed to it. You are on a journey, and because you have been distributing tracts or reading the Bible, or have made some pious observations, your fellow-travellers set you down for a Christian. By-and-by one of your companions makes a civil remark, but not being in a mood for talking, you turn him off with a short answer. A delicate passenger would like your side of the carriage, but you wish to see the country or prefer the cooler side; so you make no movement, but allow your neighbor to change places with the invalid. And at last an accident occurs which will detain you an hour beyond the usual time; so you lose all patience, and fret, and scold, and talk of hiring post-chaises,—while some good-humored or philosophic wayfarer sits quiet in the corner, or gets out, and looks leisurely on till the misfortune is mended, and then resumes his journey, having lost nothing but his time, whilst you have lost both your time and your temper. In such a case it would be better that you had left the tracts and the Bible at home, for your inconsistency is likely to do more evil, than your direct efforts are likely to do good. As a worldly man you would have been entitled to indulge your own indolence, your own convenience, or your own impatience as much as you pleased; but if you really are a disciple of Christ, you owed it to Him to "deny yourself."

The subject is uninviting, and time would fail did we speak of the parsimony, the indolence, the egotism, the want of intelligence, the want of taste, by which many excellent characters are marred, and by which the glory of the Gospel is often compromised. We would not be accusers of the brethren. We only suggest a subject for self-examination, and we indicate an object to which the Church's energy might be advantageously directed. We fear that we have failed to cultivate sufficiently the things honest, lovely, and of good report, and that we have sometimes allowed ourselves to be excelled by worldly men in those beauties of character which, though subordinate, are not insignificant. Attention to the wants of others, care for their welfare, and consideration for their feelings, are Christian graces for which all Christians ought to be conspicuous. Christianity allows us to forget our own wants, but it does not permit us to forget the necessities of our brethren. It requires us to be careless of our own ease, but it forbids us to overlook the comfort and convenience of other people. Of this the Lord Jesus was Himself the pattern. He was sometimes a-hungered, but in that case he wrought no miracle. But when the multitude had long fasted, he created bread to supply them, rather than send them away fainting. And though his great errand was to save his people from their sins, none ever saved so many from their sorrows. And in this disciples should resemble Him. Although they know that the soul is better worth than the body, and the interests of eternity more precious than those of time, they also know that it is after these things that the Gentiles seek; and, therefore, if they would win the Gentiles, they must attend to their personal wants, and temporal comforts. Nay, more, as a system of universal amelioration, Christianity demands our efforts for the outward weal of our worldly neighbors, and our delicate attention to the minutest comfort of our Christian brethren. It was on this principle that, seeking the salvation of his peasant-parishioners, Oberlin felt that he was not going out of his way as an evangelist, when he opened a school for children, wild as their own rock-goats; when he taught the older people many humble but useful arts hitherto unknown in the Ban-de-la-Roche; when he set them to the planting of trees, and clearing of roads; when he established an agricultural society, and published a calendar, divested of the astrological falsehoods with which their almanacs were wont to abound. Oberlin's Christianity would have prompted these humane and beneficent actions even though no ulterior good had accrued from them; but first in the love of these villagers, and then in their conversion to God, he had his abundant reward. And it was on the same principle that the apostolic Williams, brim-full of sense and kindness, came down like a *cornucopia* on his South Sea Islanders, and startling them with the prodigies of civilization, and enriching them with its inventions, at once conveyed an idea of the bountiful spirit of the Gospel, and conciliated their affection to its messenger. And it was on the same principle that the benignant Wilberfòrce,—himself the best "practical view of Christianity,"—was so studious of the feelings, and so accommodating to the wishes of his worldly friends,—so abounded in those considerate attentions to the humblest acquaintance, which only a delicate mind could imagine, and a dextrous skill could execute,—and would subject himself to all sorts of inconvenience in order to "carry a ray of gladness from the social circle into the sick man's cottage," or to temper with his own diffusive gladness the bitter cup of some humble disciple. No disciple can resemble his Lord, who does not maintain this benignant bearing to all around him. Grace was infused into the lips of Jesus. None in the guise of humanity was ever conscious of such power within; none ever gave outlet to inherent power in milder coruscations. His gentleness made him great; and so engaging was his aspect, so compassionate his mien, that frail mortality could lay its head securely on his bosom, though a Shekinah slept within. Believers should in this resemble Jesus. They should be mild and accessible, and, like the Sun of Righteousness, should carry such healing in their wings, as to make their very presence the harbinger of joy. It was said of Charles of Bala, that it was a good sermon to look at him. And so much of the Master's mind should reside in each disciple as to make that true of him which the old elegy says of one of England's finest worthies :—

> " A sweet attractive kind of grace,
> A full assurance given by looks,
> Continual comfort in a face
> The lineament of Gospel-books ;
> For sure that count'nance cannot lie,
> Whose thoughts are written in the eye."

LECTURE XVI.

Blunt Axes: or, Science and Good Sense.

READ ECCLES. IX. 13–18: X. 1–15.

'If the iron be blunt, and he do not whet the edge, then must he put to more strength; but wisdom is profitable to direct."

LORD BACON said, "Knowledge is power," and during the last hundred years no aphorism has been so often quoted, nor has any been so largely illustrated. In this little island, and during the present week, machinery will be in motion doing the work of five hundred millions of men; that is to say, the machines of England and Scotland will this week weave as much cloth and prepare as much food, and supply the world's inhabitants with as many commodities, as could be made by hand if all the upgrown natives of the globe were laboring night and day. Could you convert into artificers and laborers every man and woman in either hemisphere, and from the Caffres at the Cape to the Peers in our Parliament, did all agree to toil their utmost, and had they no implements besides those which primitive man possesses,—with all the expenditure of their vital powers, with all the sweat, and waste of fibre, and straining of eyesight, at the week's end it would be found that they had not done half the work, nor done that half so well as a few engines peacefully revolving under the impulse of some hogsheads of water, or so many tons of coal.

In the barbaric civilization of the old Mexicans, it was thought a wonderful exploit to transmit intelligence at the rate of 200 miles in four-and-twenty hours. As they had neither horses nor dromedaries, in order to accomplish this feat posts were established at intervals of three or four miles; and snatching the despatch from one reeking messenger, the courier burst away with it and flew over hill and valley till he reached the next station, and thrust it into the hand of another express, who, in his turn, bolted off and conveyed it farther inland, till at last it reached the Emperor. How amazed one of these old Aztecs might be could he revive from the slumber of three centuries, and see the whole accomplished without fatigue to a single human being! How amazed did he know that without shortening the breath or moistening the brow of a single messenger, communications could come and go betwixt a king and his commander-in-chief, a hundred leagues asunder, fifty times in a single day!

We see that "knowledge is power," and we constantly repeat the saying as if Bacon had been the first who remarked the strength of skill. But six-and-twenty centuries before the days of Lord Verulam, King Solomon had said, "A wise man is strong." "Wisdom is better than strength." "Wisdom is better than weapons of war." Perhaps it is owing to the imperfect sympathies which exist between theologians and philosophers, that such scriptural sayings and many others fraught with great principles have received so little justice. And hence it has come to pass that many a maxim has got a fresh circulation, and has made a little fortune of renown for its author, which is, after all, a medal fresh minted from Bible money: the gold of Moses or Solomon used up again with the image and superscription of Bacon, or Pascal, or Benjamin Franklin.

The particular example which Solomon here gives, will bring to your remembrance many parallels, from the time when Archimedes with his engines on the wall, sank the ships of Marcellus in the port of Syracuse, down to the gallant and successful defence of Antwerp conducted by the old mathematician, Carnot.* "There was a little city, and few men within it, and there came a great king against it, and besieged it, and built great bulwarks against it. Now there was found in it a poor wise man, and he by his wisdom delivered the city." And surely science is never more sublime than when thus she wins and wears the

* Livii lib. 24, cap. 34. Alison's "Europe," chap. 78.

civic crown. Or even should there be no invader at the gates, when a beneficent ingenuity is exerted to enhance the pleasures of peace; when discovery chemical or dynamical floods our streets with midnight radiance, and bids clear water spring up in the poorest attic; when it mitigates disease or multiplies the loaves of bread; when by making them nearer neighbors it forces nations to be better friends, and by diminishing life's interruptions lengthens our span of probation and our power of usefulness;—surely the "poor man" whose "wisdom" thus enriches the species deserves to sit among the princes of the people; and whilst religion should render praise to that Wonderful Counsellor who teacheth man such knowledge, patriotism and philanthropy must enrol the discoverers among the benefactors of mankind.

"Wisdom is better than strength," and the more that wisdom spreads the more human strength is saved, and the more is comfort enhanced. The bird who is about to build her nest next month will toil as long and work as hard as the sparrows and swallows who frequented the temple in the time of Solomon, and the building will be no improvement on the nests of three thousand years ago. But if Solomon's own palace were to be builded anew, modern skill could rear it much faster than Hiram's masonry; and there are few houses in London which do not contain luxuries and accommodations which were lacking in "the house of the forest of Lebanon." It is the kindness of the Creator to the inferior animal that he gives it instinct, and puts it from the outset on a plan sufficiently good for its purpose. But the prerogative of man is progress. His instincts are faint and few; whilst to reason and faith the vistas are boundless. And betwixt that "wisdom" which God has directly revealed, and those expedients which are constantly occurring to painstaking intelligence, it is so arranged that the older humanity waxes the lighter grow its toils and the more copious become the alleviations of its lot. Already a pound of coals and a pint of water will do the day's work of a sturdy man; and with a week's wages a mechanic may now procure a library more comprehensive and more edifying than that which adorned the Tusculan villa,—nay such a store of books as the wealth of Solomon could not command.

These statements meet a certain misgiving of some truly Christian minds. They love the Bible, because it is God's book. To some degree they love the landscape and the seasons, because they are God's handiwork. They can take pleasure in watching the proceedings of the lower animals, because in the dyke-building of that beaver, or the nest-building of that bird, they can mark evolutions of the all-pervading Mind. But when they come to the operations of the artisan or the architect, they are conscious of an abrupt transition, and with the poet they exclaim,

> "God made the country, but man made the town."

Here, however, there is a fallacy. So far as sinful purposes may be designed or subserved in their construction, the town and its contents are the work of man; but the materials and the skill which moulds them, are the good and perfect gifts of God. It is true that He has not taught man to make palaces and railways instinctively, as He has taught ants to build hillocks and construct covered galleries; but He has furnished the human mind with those faculties and tendencies which, under favoring circumstances, develop in railways and palaces as surely as beaver-mind develops in moles and embankments, or as bee-mind develops in combs and hexagons. And although it may be very true that the artificer is often undevout,—perhaps a libertine or an atheist; and although the curious contrivance or exquisite elaboration may be designed for any end but a holy one; when you separate the moral from the mechanical,—the sin which is man's from the skill which is Jehovah's,—in every fair product, and more especially, in every contribution to human comfort, you ought to recognize the wisdom and goodness of God as their ultimate origin no less than if you read on every object, "Holiness to the Lord," and in each artificer discerned another Aholiab or Bezaleel. The arts are the gifts of God; their abuse is from man and from the Devil. And just as an enlightened disciple looks forth on the landscape, and in its beautiful features as well as its curious ingredients, beholds mementoes of his Master; so surveying a beautiful city, its museums and its monuments, its statues and fountains; or sauntering through a gallery of arts and useful inventions, in all the symmetry of proportions and splendor of coloring, in every ingenious device and every powerful engine, he may discern the manifestations of that Mind which is wonderful in counsel and excellent in working; and so far as skill and adaptation and elegance are involved, piety will hail the Great Architect Himself as the Maker of the town.*

So Christian is art,—so truly a good gift of the Father of lights, that, wherever the Gospel proceeds, this companion should go with it.

* Those who are interested in such topics will find them fully discussed in "The Useful Arts: their Birth and Development," edited by the Rev. S. Martin.

When the missionary, Van der Kemp, was setting out for Africa, passing one of the brick-fields of London, he thought it would be such a boon to the Hottentots if he could improve their dwellings that he offered himself as a servant to the brick-maker, and spent some weeks in learning the business. And he was right. It is not easy to live godly and righteously amidst filth and darkness; and although the Gospel will not refuse to enter a Hottentot hut or an Irish cabin, when once it is admitted its tendency is to improve that cabin or hut into a cottage with tiles on the floor and glass in the windows. And, to the honor of Christian missionaries, it should be remembered that wherever they have gone they have carried those useful arts which render godliness profitable to all things. "In the schools of Sierra Leone, the girls are taught to spin and the boys to weave." In the South Sea Islands the missionaries have taught the people smiths' work and wrights' work; they have taught them to build ships and boil sugar; to print books and plant gardens. And even that race, once so besotted that its claim to the common humanity was disputed,—the Hottentots are now excellent farmers and artificers, and in the words of one of themselves, "They can make everything except a watch and a coach."*

In concluding this part of the subject I would only remark that the more things which a Christian is able to do the better. "If the axe be blunt, and he do not whet the edge, then must he put to more strength." A little skill expended in sharpening the edge, will save a great deal of strength in wielding the hatchet. But, just as the unskilful laborer who cannot handle the whetstone, must belabor the tree with a blunt instrument, and after inflaming his palms and racking his sinews, achieves less result than his neighbor whose knowledge and whose knack avail instead of brute force; so the servant who does not know the right way to do his work, after all his fatigue and fluster, will give less satisfaction

* Harris's Great Commission, pp. 196, 197. The industrial is admirably combined with the evangelistic in the French Canadian Mission, and in the Home Mission of the Presbyterian Church in Ireland.

than one who has learned the best and easiest methods; the young emigrant who has no versatility must forego many comforts which more accomplished comrades enjoy; and the householder who knows nothing of the mechanic arts, or who knows not what to do when sickness and emergencies occur, must compensate by the depths of his purse, or the strength of his arm for the defects of his skill. A blunt axe implies heavy blows and an aching arm; coarse work with a blistered hand. But "wisdom is profitable to direct." Intelligence is as good as strength, and a little skill will save both time and materials, money and temper.

Important, however, as is mechanic skill, there is a wisdom still more profitable,—a wisdom which can turn to its own account the mechanic skill of others. The clever engineer who saved the little city was a poor man, and so little understanding had his fellow-citizens, that it was with difficulty he obtained a hearing for his project, and so little gratitude had they that when the danger was past, "no one remembered the poor man." And it is sad when people have neither the skill to help themselves, nor the sense to accept the services of others. It is sad when men have neither the sagacity to devise the measures which the emergency demands, nor can so far rule their spirits as to keep "quiet" and listen to what "wise men" say. And next to his wisdom who can offer good counsel, is the wisdom of him who can take it.

"A wise man's heart is at his right hand, never off its guard."* He is calm and collected, and is not easily taken by surprise. Whereas, a fool's wits are at his left hand. His presence of mind is posthumous. He sees what he should have done when the mischief can no longer be undone. He hits on the very repartee he ought to have uttered when his assailant is already out of hearing. He suggests what would have saved the ship, when they are already raising the wreck. But, not only is it in ready resources that the fool is deficient; there is a transparent shallowness

* G. Holden.

in his vacant gaze, or self-conceited simper, and instead of that "sustained sense and gravity,"* which marks the man of mind, his garrulous egotism and confidential childishness are constantly letting out the secret of his silliness. Reserve is none of his failings. He is as frank as he is foolish; and when "he walketh by the way, his wisdom faileth him, and he saith to every one that he is a fool."

One rare manifestation of good sense is magnanimity. "If the spirit of the ruler rise up against thee, leave not thy place; for yielding pacifieth great offences." If, acting as the king's adviser, you incur his displeasure; if, in obedience to conscience, or in concern for your country, you are constrained to urge unpalatable counsel; and if your faithfulness proves offensive, instead of retiring into some other land, be patriotic, and keep your post. Instead of obeying your offended dignity and returning spleen for spleen, await the propitious season. For a soft answer turneth away wrath, and self-control will conquer your sover-

* Chalmers.

eign. Nor is it only from the ministers of despots that such sacrifice may be demanded. It extends to every official person. If you are a representative of the people, and if you are sometimes vexed and worried with unreasonable demands or ungracious remonstrances:—if you occupy some municipal station, and are brought into conflict with foul tongues and coarse natures:—if you are a member of any court, civil or ecclesiastical, where you are frequently outvoted, and measures are often carried, which you utterly abhor,—the impulse is to abdicate. Why should you serve heads so thick, and hearts so thankless? Why should you mingle with such a rabble rout, and submit day by day to have your good name kicked along the kennel? And rather than be always making motions which are lost, and protests which are laughed at, would it not be better to retire into private life, and spend your influence on those who may both take your advice and spare your feelings? True, if it were the love of praise or the love of power which put you in that post, now that popularity is waning and influence lost, by all means relinquish it. But if it were a higher motive, let the motive which took you keep you there. If it was the love of your country, or the zeal of the Gospel which drew you into office, let neither reproaches nor rough usage drive you out. Though the spirit of the populace rise up against you,—though the majority for the time overrule you, leave not your place. Calmness in the midst of contumely, equanimity under defeat will pacify great offences: and if you do not live to carry your point, when a subsequent age sees your principles triumph, you will be commemorated among the protomartyrs, who, when the cause was forlorn, labored, and never fainted.

Then, after a parenthetical reference to certain infatuations of princes, having already described the patience of wisdom, he next specifies its promptitude. "If the serpent bite before enchantment, what advantage has the charmer?" In the East, there have always been persons who, by means of music and legedermain, exert great influence over some species of serpents; so that whilst under their spell, the deadly cobra may be handled, as if he were utterly harmless. But if the charmer tread on the snake unawares, or be bitten when off his guard, he will be poisoned like another man. And to certain minds, God has given ascendency over other minds, like the influence of the serpent-charmer. Sagacious and eloquent, they are able to soothe the fury of fierce tempers, and mould rancorous natures to their will. Like David's transforming harp, as the strain advances, it looks as if a new possession had entered the exorcised frame, and a seraph smiled out at those windows, where a demon was frowning before. But alas for the harper, if Saul should snatch the javelin before David has time to touch the strings. Alas for the wise charmers! and, alas for the good cause, if the tyrant's passion towers up, or the decree of the despot goes forth before a friendly counsellor has time to interpose.

"The words of a wise man's mouth are gracious." It is a pleasure to hear him, and so enriching is his discourse, that to listen is to be wiser and better. "But the lips of a fool will swallow up himself." He is the sepulchre of his own reputation; for as long as he was silent, you were willing to give him credit for the usual share of intelligence, but no sooner does he blurt out some astounding blunder—no sooner does he begin to prattle forth his egotism and vanity, than your respect is exchanged for contempt or compassion. Nay, it is not only himself that his lips swallow up: for all unlike the "gracious" discourse of the wise man, the gossip of the fool is heartless or malignant, and often ends in "mischievous madness." From recklessness or from finding that a tale of slander will secure an audience even for a fool, he is constantly retailing calumny, and damaging other people's reputation. The rest of his talk is mere word-rubbish. "A man cannot tell what he shall be;" and, "what shall be after him, who can tell?" —such trite and irksome truisms he is retailing all the day to the sore irking of some victim ear. He is consistent. He is no wiser in deed, than in word: but even the road to the market—so patent and so frequented, he continues to miss; and in the evening he and his ass return to the farm with their unsold produce, because he had forgotten the way to the city, and would not follow his wiser companion.

Speaking as unto wise men, I would say that it is very important that Christians should be men of high accomplishment. Crowded as is the world, it has still abundant room for first-rate men; and, whosoever would ensure a welcome for society, has only to unite to good principle eminent skill in his own calling. But the day for stone hatchets and blunt axes is past, and from the humblest craft to the most intellectual profession, in order to succeed, it is requisite to be clever and active and well-informed. Doubtless, sickness and other calamities may interpose; but assuredly, no one has a right to quarrel with the world if it refuses to pay for misshapen garments and unreadable poems. And therefore I would say to my young hearers, make diligence in business, a part of your religion. Add to virtue knowledge. Whatever you intend to do, pray and study, and labor till no one can do that thing better than yourself, and then when you enter on active life, you will find that you are really wanted. And, much as you have heard of glutted markets and a redundant population, you will find that there is yet no surplus of tradesmen, or servants, or scholars, who with exalted piety combine professional excellence. Large as is the accumulation of people who through misconduct have broken down, or who through indolent mediocrity never can get on, you will find no glut of talented goodness, or of intelligence in union with principle. You will find that there is room enough for all who are really able to serve their generation.

It is especially important that those who are trying to benefit others should possess the wisdom which is profitable to direct. Much good has been defeated by the want of skill or practical wisdom in Christian professors. Many children have grown up with gloomy notions of religion from the mismanagement of parents, who so enforced its authority as to obscure its attractions. Many amiable persons have been repelled from the Gospel by the long lectures of friends who were faithful enough to reprove them, but not wise enough to win them. Many a prejudice has been created by the imprudence of one, which the exertions of many have not suffered to countervail. And many a noble enterprise, when almost safe in port, has at last been shipwrecked by well-meaning wilfulness, or through that infirmity of vision which mistakes a house-lamp for a lighthouse,—a denominational crotchet for a Christian principle.

Nor is the cultivation of sound sense unimportant with a view to personal piety.

> "That thou mayest injure no man, dove-like be,
> And serpent-like that none may injure thee."*

In a world like this, and not least in a capital like this, there is frequent need for such Christian sagacity; and wherever he lives a conscientious man must often encounter problems in conduct which tax not only all his

* Matt. x. 16, paraphrased by Cowper.

principle but all his prudence. For such exigencies there is provided a great and precious promise: "If any of you lack wisdom, let him ask of God, that giveth to all liberally, and upbraideth not; and it shall be given him." But, like all the gifts of God, this talent grows by trading; and he who prayerfully exerts his understanding in order to maintain the rightforward path of duty, will soon be fit to guide and counsel others.

LECTURE XVII.

Bread on the Waters.

"Cast thy bread upon the waters: for thou shalt find it after many days."—ECCLES. XI. 1.

WERE you going at the right season to Mysore or China, you would see thousands of people planting the corn of these countries. They sow it in the mud or on the dry soil, and then immediately they turn on a flood of water, so that the whole field becomes a shallow pond. You would think the seed was drowned. But wait a few weeks, and then go and view one of these artificial lakes, and from all its surface you will see green points rising, and day by day that grass shoots taller, till at last the water is no more seen, and till at last the standing pool has ripened into a field of rich and rustling grain. So that in its literal sense the farmers of these lands are every year fulfilling the maxim of the text. For should the spring come on them, and find their supply of rice-corn scanty, instead of devouring it all, they will rather stint themselves. They will rather go hungry for weeks together, and live on a pinched supply: for the bread which they cast on the waters this spring creates the crop on which they are to subsist next autumn and winter; and they are content to cast it on the waters now, for they are sure to find it after many days.

Or suppose that you are in the South Sea Isles, where the bread fruit grows,* and that by chance or on purpose, you scatter some of its precious bunches on the sea. At the moment you may feel that they are lost: but should the winds and waters waft them to one of those reef islands with which such seas are thickly studded, the wandering seeds may get washed ashore, and beneath those brilliant suns may quickly grow to a bread-fruit forest. And should some disasters long years after

* The cultivated sort, however, has no seeds.

wreck you on that reef, when these trees are grown and their clusters ripe, you may owe your sustenance to the bread which you cast on the waters long ago.

Such is God's husbandry. Do the right deed. Do it in faith, and in prayer commend it to the care of God. And though the waves of circumstance may soon waft it beyond your ken, they only carry it to the place prepared by Him. And whether on an earthly or a heavenly shore, the result will be found, and the reaper will rejoice that he once was a sower.

Dr. Dwight of America tells how, when the country near Albany was newly settled, an Indian came to the inn at Litchfield, and asked for a night's shelter,—at the same time confessing that from failure in hunting he had nothing to pay. The hostess drove him away with reproachful epithets, and as the Indian was retiring sorrowfully,—there being no other inn for many a weary mile,—a man who was sitting by directed the hostess to supply his wants and promised to pay her. As soon as his supper was ended, the Indian thanked his benefactor, and said he would some day repay him. Years after the settler was taken a prisoner by a hostile tribe, and carried off to Canada. However, his life was spared, though he himself was detained in slavery. Till one day an Indian came to him, and giving him a musket, bade the captive follow him. The Indian never told where they were going, nor what was his object; but day after day the captive followed his mysterious guide, till one afternoon they came suddenly on a beautiful expanse of cultivated fields, with many houses rising amongst them. "Do you know that place?" asked the Indian. "Ah, yes—it is Litchfield;" and whilst the astonished exile had not recovered his surprise and amazement, the Indian exclaimed, "And I am the starving Indian on whom at this very place you took pity. And now that I have paid for my supper, I pray you go home."

And it is to such humanities that the text has primary reference; for the context runs, "Give a portion to seven and also to eight;

for thou knowest not what evil shall be upon the earth." That is, miss no opportunity of performing kind actions. Though you should have bestowed your bounty on seven,—on a number which you might deem sufficient,—should an eighth present himself, do something for him also; for you know not what evil shall be upon the earth. You know not in this world of mutation how soon you may be the pensioner instead of the almoner. You know not how soon you may be glad of a crust from those who are at present thankful for your crumbs. Beneficence is the best insurance.

When Jonathan was young he was the heir-apparent of the throne; and in those days his favorite friend was a young Bethlehemite whom they had brought to the palace to amuse the monarch with his minstrelsy. The young Bethlehemite was brave and high-hearted, and Jonathan loved him for his genius and his lofty piety, till he and the Prince Royal were fast and firm as any brothers. At length one morning Jonathan embraced a merry boy some five years old, and donning corslet and casque he followed his own sire to the battle. Next morning their corses lay stiff on the blasted heights of Gilboa, and the young minstrel was monarch of Israel. Years passed on, and the new sovereign found himself in Saul's old palace; and whichsoever way he looked there rose upon his spirit touching memories. Here was the very throne before which he had often kneeled, harp in hand, and watched the grim tyrant's features; and there was the wainscot in which his furious javelin had hung and quivered. And now he trode again the terraces where he and Jonathan had paced together, and sworn eternal friendship as they dreamed out a radiant future. He visited again the field in which they had set up their target and contended in friendly rivalry. He visited again the bower in which they took sweet counsel, and where they sang "The Lord is my Shepherd," and "Make a joyful noise," while yet these psalms were new. And everything brought back that pure and noble friend so tenderly, that the whole soul of the sovereign yearned for some living relic on whom to lavish his regretful fondness. "And is there none?" No, none; except this feeble limping youth, the little boy that was, and who dates his lameness from his father's funeral. Yes, but fetch him! Fetch Mephibosheth. He is all of Jonathan which now survives on earth; and for his dear father's sake, he shall have again all his patrimony, and, if he must not be the King, he shall never eat bread at meaner board than mine. And as he looked on the countenance so mnemonic of one yet dearer; and as he rejoiced to see the poor youth reinstated in that home of which he was the natural heir; and as he eyed Mephibosheth filling in the banquet-hall the place which Jonathan had filled, whilst as yet himself was but a menial, David could sing with much significance, "I have been young and now am old; yet have I not seen the righteous forsaken, nor his seed begging bread. He is even merciful and lendeth, and his seed is blessed." And David's own son, when he saw that sight,—when he saw Jonathan's old kindness requited in this princely provision for his child,—Solomon might say, as here he says, "Cast thy bread on the waters, and thou shalt find it after many days."

Although so often exemplified in cases of common humanity and kind-heartedness, the maxim of our text is especially applicable to the effects of Christian philanthropy. These are pre-eminently amaranthine. There are seeds which, after being borne on the current for a few days or weeks lose their vitality; they rot and sink and disappear. So is it with much of human effort. So is it with many a worldly scheme, many a plausible suggestion, many a patriotic enterprise. It finds little favor in its day; it cannot get deposited in a sufficient number of appropriate minds; and so, ere long, it becomes old and obsolete; the thought perishes, the seed rots and disappears. But not so with pious efforts. It is more than the lucky thought of fallible and short-sighted man; it is more than the well-meaning purpose of a feeble and sinful worm. It is a thought suggested by God's own Spirit; it is a purpose sustained and animated by One whose wisdom is infinite and who is alive for evermore. And though the mind in which that wish or effort first originated may long since have passed from these scenes of mortality,—though forgetful of its cunning, the hand which first launched on the tide of human thought that project or that principle, may long since be crumbling in the clay, a heavenly life is at its core, and as it journeys on its buoyant path a covenant God will keep alive its little ark till it reach the predestined creek, and after many days be drawn forth from the waters,—the Moses of the mind.

So was it with the first Reformers. Searching in their Bibles they found truths of God which had vanished from the memories of men,—great truths and glorious, no longer current in the vernacular of Christendom. But after their own understandings and hearts had been filled and expanded by them, they gave them utterance. That it is through the justified Surety that a sinner is just with God; that betwixt that sinner and that Surety nothing mediates nor intervenes, neither Mary in heaven nor mother Church on earth, neither the sainted mediator of the Calendar nor the sacerdotal mediator of the Confessional, but that to his great High Priest, the God-man, Immanuel, the sinner may come boldly and may come direct; that in order to receive the atonement and rejoice in Christ Jesus no preliminaries of penance, or pilgrimages, are requisite, but that for this great salvation, sin is sufficient fitness, and the Word and will of God sufficient warrant; these and other golden truths, fresh gleaned from the Bible, they published, some preaching them from pulpits, some proclaiming with their pens. And the hosts of darkness took alarm. Wickliffe went to the dungeon; Huss and Jerome to the funeral pile. But though the witnesses perished the Word of God could not be bound: the truth of God was neither bound, burned, nor buried: but over the troubled deep of a dark and stormy century this bread of life, these seeds of saving knowledge floated on, till God the Spirit landed them and planted them in minds prepared, and from these rescued waifs there sprung the glorious Reformation.

It were only to tell the same tale a little varied to rehearse how once upon a time every enterprise of Christian charity was once a project in some solitary and prayerful mind; and how when cast forth on the waters of thought and opinion, it first halted and hovered and looked as if it would never get to sea: and how, after touching at one point after another, and finding momentary favor only to be rebuffed again, some great gulf-current swept it clean away, and its author hoped to see it no more. And away it went; and it was bandied on the billows and it was battered on the rocks, and it was froze in the iceberg, and it was roasted in the tropic, till at last the Eye that watched it and the Hand that steered it from above, conducted it to its sunny haven, and safely landed on an honest soil, it burst and bourgeoned and waxed a mighty tree.

So understood, the principle admits of boundless application; and should be very cheering to all who are engaged in labors of Christian love. For instance, if you are engaged in teaching your own children, or the children of other people, and your great anxiety is to see some good thing towards the Lord—some dawn of pious feeling, some development of personal earnestness; but notwithstanding all the endearment which you throw into your words, and all the prayer with which you follow up your instructions, you dare hardly say that you perceive any hopeful sign. Never mind. It is God's own truth, and if all your heart be in it, it is living truth, and will blossom up some day. It may be in that soul's salvation out and out. It may be in restraining it much from sin, or in urging it to duties which it would otherwise have never thought of doing,—and it may be after many days. It may be after your own day altogether. It may be on the shores of another continent. It may be on the shores of another world. But still, God's Word shall not go forth a living power, and come back a vacant nullity. That word shall never go forth without returning, and when it returns it shall never be void.

"In the morning, then, sow thy seed, and in the evening withhold not thy hand: for thou knowest not which shall prosper, this or that, or whether both shall be alike good."

LECTURE XVIII.

Know thy Mercies.

Read Eccles. ii. 24–26; iii. 12, 13, 22; v. 18–20; viii. 15; ix. 7–10.

"I know that there is no good in them, but for a man tc rejoice, and to do good in his life. And also that every man should eat and drink, and enjoy the good of all his labor: it is the gift of God."

Every moment brings its mercy; why should not mercies bring content? To the man who finds favor in his sight, God gives "wisdom and knowledge." He is conscious of his comforts, and he has sense to use them. But to the sinner God gives "travail." He has the toil of acquirement without the power of enjoyment. "There is nothing better for a man than that he should eat and drink, and that he should make his soul enjoy good in his labor."

Throughout the whole of the book language like this is constantly recurring. And, without pausing to enter a caveat against Epicurian perversions of the sentiment, we may at once proceed to its legitimate applications. Of all philosophies the most eclectic is evangelical Christianity; and many a sentiment which, isolated, would be an error, is not only innocent but useful, when acting as a tributary to this master principle.

Even in the days of his vanity, Solomon "saw" that there would be more happiness if there were less hankering. He saw it in mankind; he suspected it in himself. Like the November bee, with its forehead smeared in the honey of the hive, and which, smelling that deceitful lure, fancies that it is the nectar of far-off flowers, and which still scenting somewhere ahead a land of honey, flies farther and farther a-field, till the evening mist enshrouds it and congeals upon its wings, and drags it benumbed to the frozen furrow; so Solomon had often seen his neighbors flying far into the winter in search of that honey which they had left at home; and he said, It would have been better that they had "eaten and drunken," from the produce of their previous toil;—it would have been better if, instead of always laboring after more, they could have halted, and enjoyed the good "of their former labor."

And surely this principle is of extensive application. Without disparaging the pleasures of hope, or seeking to quell the zeal of progress, are the cases not numberless where, for all purposes of enjoyment, labor is lost, because coupled with the constant lust of farther acquirement? or because of a strange oblivion of his own felicity on the part of the favored possessor?

Behold us here in Britain, near the middle month of the nineteenth century, surrounded with the broadest zone of peace and material comfort to be found in all the map of history. Looking at our temporal lot, we of this generation and this country, stand on the very pinnacle of outward advantage; in all our lives never once affrighted by the rumor of invasion; exempt from all the horrors of impressment and conscription; ignorant of martyrdoms religious and political;—free, self-governed, independent. Who knows it? Who remembers it? Who in these matters adverts to his own happiness? As she presses to her bosom her little boy, or parts on his open brow the darkening hair amidst all her maternal pride, where is the mother who praises God for her young Briton's privilege? How many hearts remember to swell with the joyful recollection, Thank God, he may leave me if he pleases; but he can never be dragged from me against his will! He may become a More among lawyers, a Latimer among preachers, a Sidney among statesmen, and need dread neither stake nor scaffold. He may become the victim of false accusation and malignant persecution; but he will not languish, without trial, slow years in a dungeon, nor by the rack befrenzied into a false witness against himself. He may turn out unwise, he may turn out unhappy; but, thank God, the son of British sire can never feel the tyrant's torture in his limbs, nor the brand of slavery on his brow!

Behold that home of yours! What an Eden a thankful heart might make it! What a concentration of joys it will appear, as soon as the Spirit, the Comforter, has revealed its brightness; or as soon as its little groups and its daily scenes can only be viewed in the pictures of gold and ebony which furnish the mourner's memory! And yet, how often does your own peevishness embitter all its joy: and how often, with foolish hankering, do you quit its hoarded pleasures, and fly away to clubs and crowded rooms, to theatres, or lonely travel, in search of the honey you have left at home!

Behold your position as a candidate for immortality! What could you desire which the God of grace has not done for you already? A salvation more complete, a Bible more plain, a revelation more abundant? And yet, instead of sitting down contentedly and thankfully to this "feast of fat things," and abandoning yourself to all the blessedness which is so freely given you, do you not usually find a barrier of dilatoriness or distrust rising up betwixt you and the costly provision? With that Gospel spreading blandly before you, there is nothing better for you than to eat and drink of its mercies, and enjoy the good which it brings you. Oh, study to realize your amazing position, as one whom Jehovah all-sufficient is daily inviting into his friendship, and whom the wearer of a sinless humanity is willing to call his brother. Fear not to think it, that to you, poor tenant of the dust, a white robe and a golden harp are offered. Fear not to think it, all sin-laden and sin-pervaded as you are, that to the fellowship of angels and his own society, the Holy One invites you. Fear not to think it, that as a believer in Jesus, and so a member of his great ransomed body, your very self is soon to be an inhabitant of that world where there is neither sin nor sorrow, and a burgess of that city whose streets are gold, and whose gates are pearl. Fear not to think such things; but fear to forget them. Fear not to believe such things; but fear to credit them in a cold and vacant manner. Fear to get into that habit which engulfs any amount of God's mercies as the ocean engulfs the argosie, without feeling richer or fuller, or giving any revenue back.

One great source of our prevailing joylessness is our inadvertency. Living in Rome, a famous antiquarian and artist* tells us that he gave himself half an hour every day to meditate on his Italian happiness. There was wisdom in the rule. Thousands have lived in Rome, with the same pure sky smiling over them and the same articulate antiquity on every side accosting them, and never been aware of their felicity; just as there are thousands who growl and grumble through long years of English life, and never bless God for the greater mercy of being born in Britain. Few of us need to be better off—we all need to know how well off we are. We need to meditate on our human happiness. We might have been lost angels, of whose race no Redeemer took hold. We might have been cut

* Winkelman.

off in our sins long ago, and now be in the place where God forgetteth to be gracious. We might have been born in dark or despotic lands, where faith is a miracle, and where piety is a martyrdom. We might have labored under those prejudices of education which make belief in the faithful saying, as hard as it is for a camel to pass through the eye of a needle. Then absolutely: there is for our meditation, daily, hourly, life-long, God's chief mercy,—that largess of unprecedented love which is not the envied distinction of some far-off world, but is God's gift unspeakable to you, to me. Oh, let us for once dwell on our peerless prerogative, till we become a wonder to ourselves,—till but for our faith in God we would not be able to believe our own distinguished blessedness. "This is the record that God hath given to us eternal life, and this life is in his Son." "He that hath the Son hath life." "He that spared not his own Son, but delivered him up for us all, how shall he not with him freely give us all things?" "Who is he that condemneth? It is Christ that died, yea, rather, that is risen again, who is even at the right hand of God, who also maketh intercession for us." "Bless the Lord, O my soul, and all that is within me, bless his holy name: who forgiveth all thine iniquities, —who healeth all thy diseases,—who redeemeth thy life from destruction, — who crowneth thee with loving-kindness and tender mercies."

Another source of depression is distrustfulness. Am I wrong, my friends? Are not some of you in this predicament? You have no particular evil to record against the past, and yet you have great fears for the future. If you be a Christian, on the whole your life has been a happy one,—and yet with all that past happiness, you are afraid that you cannot be so happy hereafter. You are afraid that grief is coming—all the more afraid that grief is coming because so much joy is past. But this is wrong. This is perverse reasoning. If a child of God, your greatest happiness is coming yet. You are going up into a future where mightier than the mightiest trial—a grief-transforming, cloud-dispelling Friend awaits you. If God be your chiefest good, and conformity to God be your great desire, the future contains no real evil for you. In that future there may await you some painful incidents. The loss of this and that other loved one may await you there,—the loss of your substance,—the loss of your health may await you, *and they may not;* sufficient unto the day is the evil thereof. But whatever else is in store for you, if you go piously and prayerfully forward into that future, you will find that many sweet mercies are there awaiting you,—many blessings at this moment unsurmised and unsuspected,—blessings, some of them, which the mourner only knows; and you will find that in that future God awaits you, as present, as powerful, and as kind as He has been in the most favored past. So, summon up courage and go cheerfully forward. "Hope in the Lord; for with the Lord there is mercy." And whatever else you limit, set no limits to the loving-kindness of the Lord, nor to the largeness of those petitions by which the needy suppliant honors the liberal Giver. Many indulge a complaining spirit who scarcely reflect how wicked it is, and how provoking to the Most High. They take up the Bible, and they read the murmurings of Israel on the march to Canaan, and they pity poor Moses, and they do not wonder that, wearied with their petulance and peevishness, the Lord smote these rebels, so that all their carcasses fell in the wilderness. And when they have read the narrative, they close the book; and the first member of the family that comes in their way, they have ready a long lecture of rough reprimanding and perverse fault-finding; or the first visitor that arrives, they inflict on him the story of their grievances; they tell how good and meritorious they have been, but how severely the Lord has frowned upon their wishes, and how cruelly the Lord has baffled all their plans. Yes, brethren, we marvel at old Israel, because we are ignorant of ourselves. If, just as Canaan was the prize of meekness, and a single murmur was enough to forfeit it,—if the Lord suspended any blessing on the same condition,—if those only were to find next year prosperous who never grumbled this one, and those only were to get to heaven who never murmured by the way, which of us,—who of all the two millions of London, would be the modern Joshua and Caleb? And yet, as it is, who would not try? Who is there that would not court the panegyric which God pronounced on the sons of Nun and Jephunneh? Who is there that would not wish the perpetual feast of a contented spirit, and the perpetual ornament of a praising one? Let us, brethren, combat our natural fault-finding, and our no less natural foreboding. Let us rejoice in the present, and let us trust for the future. Let us pray and strive till our frame of mind is more in unison with the Lord's kindness; and in the fulfilment of any wish and the disappointment of any fear,—in the kindness of any friend, and in the answer to any prayer, —in every gracious providence, and in every spiritual mercy bestowed on ourselves or others dear,—in all these let us recognize the merciful kindness of the Lord, and let us acknowl edge what we recognize. "It is a good thing to give thanks unto the Lord, and to sing praises unto thy name, O Most High: to show forth thy loving-kindness in the morning, and thy faithfulness every night; for thou, Lord, hast made me glad through thy work: I will triumph in the works of thy hands."

LECTURE XIX.

Old Age.

READ ECCLES. XII. 1–7.

"Remember thy Creator, . . . while the evil days come not, nor the years draw nigh, when thou shalt say, I have no pleasure in them."

A DISSIPATED youth is sure to be followed by a cross and joyless old age. During the years of his ungodliness, Solomon had been a fast liver, and, most likely, he now felt creeping over him the jejune and dreary feelings which foretell a premature decline. No dew of youth survived to create a green old age, and having forestalled the reserve of strength and spirits, he had failed withal to lay up against this time a good foundation of faithful friends and pleasant memories. The portrait is general; but an old worldling seems to have supplied the original.

Of his last years this old man says, "I have no pleasure in them." Once on a time existence was a joy, and the exuberant spirits overflowed in shouts and songs and hilarious ditties. So abundant was the joy of life that, like the sunbeams in a tropic clime, it was needful to shade it, and with a Venetian lattice of imagined sorrows and tragic tales the young man assuaged the over-fervid beams of his own felicity.

"In youth he loved the darksome lawn,
Brushed by the owlet's wing;
Then twilight was preferred to dawn,
And autumn to the spring.

Sad fancies did he then affect,
In luxury of disrespect
To his own prodigal excess
Of too familiar happiness." *

Now there is no need of such artificial abatements. It is not easy for the old man to get a nook so warm that it will thaw the winter in his veins. To say nothing of a song, it is not

* Wordsworth.

easy for him to muster up a smile; and as he listens with languid interest to the news of the day, and, in subtle sympathy with his own failing faculties, as he disparages this modern time and its dwindled men, it is plain that, as for the world, its avocations and amusements, its interests and its inhabitants, he has little pleasure in them.

It adds to the evil of such days that the pleasures of expectation are constantly lessening. Old age is a Terra del Fuego,—a region where the weather never clears. Once when a trivial ailment came, the hardy youth could outbrave it, and still go on with his daily duties. But now, every ailment is important, and they are never like to end. The cough is cured only to be succeeded by an asthma, and when the tender eyes have ceased to trickle, the ears begin to tingle. Once upon a time a few drops might fall into the brightest day, like a settling shower in June; and there were apt to be hurricanes, equinoctial gales, great calamities, drenching and devastating sorrows. But now, the day is all one drizzle, and life itself the chief calamity, and there is little space for hope where the weather is all either clouds or rain.

Then in the third and three following verses, there is given an allegorical sketch of the infirmities of age. "The keepers of the house tremble." Those arms once so brawny wither. The Priam who could have cleft a brazen panoply, can now fling a spear with scarce an infant's force,—and the David who could hurl his pebble straight into the centre of Goliath's brow, can scarcely carry to his own lips a cup of water. In either arm the sturdy champion used to feel that he had two stout defenders,—two trusty keepers of the castle; but now that he is old, any one can bind them and carry him whither he would not. "And the strong men bow themselves." Those active limbs can do no more. The pedestrian tells how once on a time he walked his hundred miles in four-and-twenty hours, and then, as he gets up to give a specimen, he stumbles on the carpet. That other disciple who outran Peter can no longer creep from his couch to the sanctuary, but is fain to be carried in his chair. Be thankful, Asahel, that you die so soon, or none would believe that your feet were once swifter than a roe. Be thankful, Samson, that you perish in your prime, or it would not have been easy to believe that these bending legs of yours once bore the gates of Gaza. "The strong men bow themselves, and the grinders cease because they are few." The daily meal is itself a drudgery; for the teeth have fallen out, and the masticating process is a fatigue and a trouble. And, still sorer privation, the eyes are dim. "Those that look out of the windows are darkened." The landscape is a blot,—the very world is misty. The writer's inkhorn is allowed to dry, and the virtuous woman who clothed all her household with scarlet,—her needles now rust in the unopened case. And whatever may have been the pleasure derived from works of information or of fancy, that pleasure has faded; for, except in the brief winter's noon, the eye can no longer decipher the wavering lines, and even though by reading aloud, friendship endeavors to supply their failures, the effort is defeated by the dulness of the ear. "The doors are shut in the streets." Soft sounds no longer get in; and though by bawling lustly, a son or a daughter may ask or answer some occasional question,—poor substitute these volleyed and intermitting utterances,—poor substitute for the whispers of affection, and the sweet accents of familiar voices, and that calm, effortless participation in all the passing converse which were the privilege of happier days. But, not only is the door of audience closed, the door of utterance is also shut. "The grinders have ceased," and with lips collapsed and organs all impaired, it is an effort to talk; and bending silently in on his own solitude, the veteran dozes in his elbow-chair the long summer hours when younger folks are busy. But if he dozes in the day, he does not sleep at night. At the voice of the bird, at the crowing of the cock, although he does not hear it, he can keep his couch no longer. He rises whilst industry is still locked in needed slumber, and even before the sleep-cloud has melted from the eyes of infancy. He rises, but not because he has any work to do, or any pleasure to enjoy. "He is afraid of that which is high, and fears are in the way." He has neither enterprise nor courage. Once it was a treat to press up the mountain side and enjoy the majestic prospect. Now, there is no high place which is not formidable; and even to the temple it is a sad drawback that it stands on Zion, and that it is needful to "go up." "The almond-tree flourishes, and the grasshopper is burdensome." Tease him not with your idle affairs. In that load of infirmities he has encumbrance enough to carry, and though it be not the weight of a feather, do not augment his burden, who totters under the load of many years. For "desire has failed." You can grapple with heavy tasks,—you can submit to severe toil and protracted self-denial, for you have a purpose to serve—you have an end in view,—you have an inducement which countervails toil and cheats the self-denial. But with him there is no inducement, for there is no ulterior. "Desire has failed." "Barzillai, come and live with me at the palace," says

David. And, answers Barzillai, "I am this day fourscore years old; can I discern between good and evil? Can thy servant taste what I eat or what I drink? Can I hear any more the voice of singing men and singing women? Let thy servant, I pray thee, turn back, that I may die in my own city, and be buried in the grave of my father and of my mother." Yes, that is all of "desire" that now remains,—the desire to die at home, and be buried in the family grave. And it is presently fulfilled. For now the old man goes to his long home, and his funeral walks the streets. The other morning his children came and found nothing but the ruin. The silver cord by which it was suspended had worn out at last, and the lamp of life was fallen to the ground,—the lights extinguished and the golden bowl which fed them broken.* The pitcher was shattered beside the fountain, and the cistern wheel demolished. The eye was glass. The heart was still. And now dust goes back to dust,—for the soul has already gone to the God who gave it.

* Noyes.

This description gives great emphasis to the exhortation of the outset. Remember thy Creator in youth—for if you do not remember Him then, your next leisure will be old age, and now you see what sort of leisure that is. How foolish to calculate on a time which not one youth in ten ever sees! How fatal to calculate on a time which, were it really come, you could turn to no account! Suppose that by an interposition of Omnipotence, you were lifted over the interval of years. Suppose that you, who are this day fifteen, were to awake to-morrow and find yourself fourscore. You know what it is to be very sleepy, and how tiresome it is to have people talking to you when you can scarcely keep open your eyes. You know what it is to be very sad, and when your heart is breaking, you know how painful it is to be obliged to go about your daily tasks, and how little progress you make in this disconsolate diligence. You know what it is to be very sick; and if, when you cannot lift your head from the pillow, your little sister were bringing in lilies of the valley or new wall-flowers of the spring, you would look languidly at it, and soon put it away; or if they asked you to rise and take a ride, you would feel that they were mocking you. So is it with old age. It is drowsy, and sad, and full of infirmity; and to go to an old man who has never minded religion in his youth—to go to him and ask him to mind it now, would be like singing songs to a heavy heart; it would be like telling stories to a sleepy man; it would be like showing pictures or presenting nosegays to a tortured invalid. And were you now waking up to a sudden old age, you would find all over you a strange stupor: the windows darkened, and the street-doors closed. And you would find yourself very dull. These are days when you would say, "I have no pleasure in them." And like a man constantly in a dim disease, you would feel as if you never were hale enough to throw all your heart into the subject. And when pious friends pressed you and entreated you to think of your soul, you would pray them, "I cannot attend. Everything fatigues me now. The grasshopper is a burden. I know that the subject is awfully important. So much the worse for me—for I cannot take interest in anything. Desire has failed. My heart is weary—my soul is dim. Oh, leave me, leave me to repose!" O my dear young friends, give the Saviour your heart whilst you have a heart to give. Listen to his voice whilst your feelings still are fresh, and give Him your affections before your natures grow dry and arid.

For this is our next lesson: The Creator remembers in their old age, those who in youth remember Him. This is a woful picture, but some of the features would scarcely be recognized in an old disciple. At least it cannot be truly said by an aged Christian, "I have no pleasure;" and though there may be "clouds," he has also long and sunny intervals, and beyond this cloudy region he has blessed prospects. The peace which the Saviour gives to his people, is a well of water springing up unto everlasting life; and there is nothing which keeps the feelings so fresh and youthful as a perennial piety. "Even the youth shall faint and be weary, and the young men shall utterly fall." The young men of this world must grow old; and a few years hence the young man rejoicing in his youth shall be leaning on his staff for very feebleness. "But they that wait upon the Lord shall renew their strength." And if you want to know the difference between animal and spiritual youth, just compare that young spendthrift who bows his head like a bulrush, because he is conscious of debt and dishonesty and the disrespect of all around; compare him with that old, but frugal and contented saint, who carries his head erect as the palm-tree, and who, like the palm-tree, has constant sunshine on it. Compare that young profligate who, after a night of riot, is now dragging his reluctant steps to his hated post, and with bleared eyes and throbbing temples, is yawning forth his vacancy, or ejaculating his chagrin;—compare him with yon serene and cheerful Christian who, now that life's working-day is over, is resting from his labors for a little before he passes to his reward, and whose evening is so bright that the youngest are glad to come forth and bask in its beams. Compare that young skeptic who has half persuaded himself into the disbelief of God and hereafter,—and whose forced unbelief is often interrupted by intrusions of unwelcome conviction,—compare him with Paul the aged in prison, writing, "I know whom I have believed. I am now ready to be offered, and the time of my departure is at hand; I have fought a good fight, I have finished my course, I have kept the faith. Henceforth, there is laid up for me a crown of righteousness, which the Lord, the righteous Judge, shall give me at that day."

It is not very long ago since the lives of two veterans appeared so simultaneous as almost to compel the contrast. Their declining days were somewhat similar. When getting old and feeling frail, they lost some of their dearest friends, and each lost his fortune. In these circumstances Sir Walter writes, "I used to think a slight illness was a luxurious thing. . . . . . It is different in the latter stages—the old post-chaise gets more shattered at every turn; windows will not pull up, doors refuse to open, or being open, will not shut again. There is some new subject of complaint every moment—your sicknesses come thicker and thicker; your sympathizing friends fewer and fewer. The recollection of youth, health, and uninterrupted powers of activity, neither improved nor enjoyed, is a poor strain of comfort. Death has closed the long dark avenue upon loves and friendships; and I look at them as through the grated door of a burial-place filled with monuments of those who were once dear to me, with no insincere wish that it may open for me at no distant period, provided such be the will of God. I shall never see the threescore and ten, and shall be summed up at a discount. No help for it, and no matter either."* Recovering from a similar slight illness, Mr. Wilberforce remarked, "I can scarce understand why my life is spared so long, except it be to show that a man can be as happy without a fortune as with one." And

* "Scott's Life," Second Edition, vol. ix. pp. 60, 61.

then, soon after, when his only surviving daughter died, he writes, "I have often heard that sailors on a voyage will drink, 'Friends astern,' till they are half-way over, then 'Friends a-head.' With me it has been 'friends a-head' this long time."*

Precious in the sight of the Lord is the death of his saints; and God's kindness to his aged servants is often displayed in their gentle dismissal. In view of advancing years it has been sweetly and cheerfully sung by an English poetess:—†

"Life! we've been long together,
Through pleasant and through cloudy weather.
'Tis hard to part when friends are dear,
Perhaps 'twill cost a sigh, a tear;
Then steal away, give little warning,
Choose thine own time;
Say not good night, but in some happier clime,
Bid me good morning."

And the boon has oft been vouchsafed to the mature and Simeon-like disciple. Many of you remember "Father" Wilkinson, who preached the Golden Lecture so many years

* "Wilberforce's Life," vol. v. pp. 326, 328.

† Mrs. Barbauld.

in London. One evening he told his daughter that he had long dreaded dying in his sleep, and that he had nightly prayed that it might not be so: "But this night," he added, "I have withdrawn that petition, and will leave this and all my matters in God's hands." It was the last link of bondage broken: the last fibre of self-will uprooted; and having thus completed his meetness, the Lord surprised his servant into blessedness that self-same night. Last week we read a similar instance of a veteran's gentle home-going. In the days of Gallican persecution, Pastor Faber sat at the table of the Queen of Navarre one afternoon, when some other Protestant refugees were present. He was looking sad, and when they asked the reason he replied with tears, "I am now a hundred years old, and when many young men are sealing their testimony with their blood, here have I, the craven, saved myself by flight." The Queen and her friends assured him that in consulting his own safety he had only fulfilled his Lord's command; and by-and-by he brightened up, and said,

"Then nothing remains but that I go back to God; for I perceive that He calls me. But, first, if you please, I shall make my will." Then turning his eyes on the Queen he said, "I constitute you my executrix and residuary legatee. My books I bequeath to M. Gerard, the Preacher. My clothes and whatever else I have I give to the poor. The rest I commit to God." At which the Queen smiling, asked, "Yes, but, James, what will revert to your residuary legatee?" "The charge of dispensing to the poor," he answered. "And I," exclaimed her Majesty, "accept it, and I vow that it is to me a more grateful heritage than if my royal brother had bequeathed to me the kingdom of France." Thereupon the old man, saying that he wanted rest, bade the guests a cheerful good-night and retired into an adjoining chamber. They thought that he was sleeping, and so he was. He had fallen asleep in a palace, and he awoke in heaven.*

My young friends, let me claim your kindness for the old. They are well entitled to

" Witsii Miscellanea Sacra, tom. ii. p. 184.

your sympathy. Through this bright world they move mistily, and though they rise as soon as the birds begin to sing, they cannot hear the music. Their limbs are stiff, their senses dull, and that body which was once their beautiful abode and their willing servant, has become a cage and a heavy clog. And they have outlived most of those dear companions with whom they once took sweet counsel.

> " One world deceas'd, another born,
> Like Noah they behold,
> O'er whose white hairs and furrow'd brows
> Too many suns have roll'd."*

Make it up to them as well as you can. Be eyes to the blind, and feet to the lame. On their way to the sanctuary be their supporting staff, and though it may need an extra effort to convey your words into their blunted ear, make that effort;—for youth is never so beautiful as when it acts as a guardian angel, or a ministering spirit to old age. And should extreme infirmity or occasional fretfulness try

* Young.

your patience, remember that to all intents you were once the same, and may be the same again;—in second childhood, as in first, the debtor of others' patience and tenderness and magnanimity.

And, my aged friends, let me commend you to the sympathy of the Saviour. The merciful High Priest knows your frame. The dull ear and the dim eye are no obstacles to intercourse with Him; and the frequent infirmities prayer can convert into pleas for his compassion. "What are you doing?" said a minister, as he one day visited a feeble old man, who dwelt in a windy hovel. "What are you doing?" as he saw him sitting beneath the dripping rafters in his smoky chamber, with his Bible open on his knee. "Oh, Sir! I am sitting under his shadow with great delight, and his fruit is sweet to my taste!" That is dainty food which even Barzillai might discern. Feed upon its promises; draw water from its wells of salvation. And when one sight after another fades away from your darkening eyes, look more and more to Jesus;—

for if He be your joy, your hope, your life, the faster you are clothed with the snows of eld, the sooner will you renew your youth in the realms of immortality.

> " In age and feebleness extreme,
> Who shall a helpless worm redeem?
> Jesus my only hope Thou art,
> Strength of my failing flesh and heart;
> O, could I catch a smile from Thee,
> And drop into eternity!"

LECTURE XX.

The Wicket-gate.

"Let us hear the conclusion of the whole matter: Fear God, and keep his commandments: for this is the whole of man."—ECCLES. XII. 13.

GOD is Almighty. Some beings concentrate in themselves a large amount of power. Some of our fellow-mortals have possessed so much vital energy,—minds so inventive and vigorous as to leave their impress on a realm or on a continent; and when you ask, Who engineered this road? who devised this law? who erected this monument? you are amazed to find everywhere the trace of one imperial intellect. But ascend into Heaven or plunge into Hades,—take the wings of the morning and visit the farthest isles of Immensity, and there is one Presence which will still rivet you, and one great footstep which still you must fail to measure. Who made this worm which grovels in the clay? who made yon seraph who hovers round the Light of lights? Who lit the glow-worm's taper? who filled with bright millenniums the sphery lamp of yonder sun? Who gives this dancing atom its afternoon of life? who is it that has kindled immortality in the soul of man? Who is it that fills that hive with industry, that home with peaceful joy, that heaven with adoring ecstasy? The Alpha and Omega, the first and the last, who is and was and is to come, the Almighty.

God is all-wise. When as yet nothing existed except the great I Am, to his infinite understanding all combinations of existence were present. They stood forth so many beautiful and Divine ideas, and from this panopticon of all the possible his holy wisdom chose the best, and willed that universe which is. And now that alongside of all the past his boundless comprehension includes the farthest future, each evolving incident owes its being to that Providence which is particular because it is universal; and nothing comes into existence which is a surprise to Omniscience, or which does not instantly find its place prepared in the glorious whole: so that from the falling sparrow to the dying martyr, and from the fortunes of some poor human family to the events of an incarnation, all history is an anthem ascribing "to the King eternal, immortal, invisible, THE ONLY WISE GOD," "honor and glory forever and ever."

God is all-holy. He is the infinite Excellence. That river of pleasures which makes glad the celestial city, is just so much of his goodness as God is pleased to reveal; but the full fountain remains in Jehovah himself,—an ocean which Gabriel's line cannot fathom, and athwart which the archangel's wing cannot traverse,—an abyss of brightness of which immensity alone is the margin, and of which each holy intelligence is but a sparkling drop. Yet, little as our searching can find out God, we know that his name is just the highest name for goodness and blessedness. We know that his is the mind to which evil is the supreme impossibility. We know that he is the God of truth, and without iniquity: just and right is He. Amidst the multitude of promises which his munificence has prompted him to make, we know that not one good word hath failed, but every yea has found its Amen. Amidst the multitude of creatures over which his sovereignty extends, we know that there exists no instance of unkindness, or neglect, or oppression. And amidst the multitude of thoughts and emotions which make up the joys of Deity, we know that there is not one malevolent affection; but all is condescension to his creatures, care for their well-being, and delectation in their joy.

But if God be the only good and the all-inclusive joy, a creature's blessedness must consist in a right relation and a right emotion towards Him. To be separated from the supreme felicity, must itself be misery; and to entertain unkind or hostile feelings towards infinite excellence, must itself be the deepest depravity.

What then is a right relation to God? It is that coincidence with his good pleasure, and that compliance with his revealed will which Solomon calls "keeping his commandments." He is our Creator, or whether we will or will not, we must be his creatures. But he is also the King of the universe, and we ought to be his loyal subjects. And in Christ Jesus he is prepared to become our Father, and we should reciprocate the matchless condescension, and with wonder and astonishment exclaiming, "Our Father which art in heaven," we should become the sons and daughters of the Lord God Almighty.

And what is the right feeling towards God? Almighty and all-wise, we should devoutly adore Him. Our righteous Ruler, we should with cheerful submission acquiesce in his disposal, and with strenuous activity should fulfil his commands. Our kind and merciful Father, we should give him unhesitating love and confidence without reserve. And altogether, did we realize his perfections and our own position, it would become our "chief end to glorify God and to enjoy Him forever."

Many, however, will feel that the great difficulty lies in getting into this right relation. Allowing it to be the creature's blessedness to glorify and enjoy the Creator, how shall a sinful creature begin to taste this blessedness? How shall I assure myself that the Most High is no longer offended with me? And how shall I bring myself to that state in which my Creator shall be able to regard me with habitual complacency? Is the process very arduous and very long? Must I relinquish my present calling and give myself wholly to the business of working out my peace with God? Had I not better retire into a desert or a hermitage? And how long will the ordeal last? In how many months or years may I begin to hope that God is propitious, and that heaven will be mine?

Some people once lived in a Happy Isle, but for their misdeeds they had been banished. Their place of exile was a cheerless coast; but it lay within distant sight of their former home.

Soon after their expulsion a message had come from their injured Sovereign, offering to all who pleased an amnesty. Few minded it. They had grown sour and sullen, and they tried to persuade themselves that the earth-holes in which they burrowed, were more comfortable than the mansions of his land, and that the mallows among their bushes were more nutritious than all the fruits of his gardens. One man, however, was of a different mind. He was a musing, thoughtful person. Often might you have seen him pacing the beach when the rays of evening shone on the Happy Isle, and whilst the sea-bird wailed over his head and the wrack crackled under his feet, from his own dreary prison he wistfully eyed the forests on its coast, and the mountains of purple streaked with silver which sate enthroned on its interior; and as he fancied that he could sometimes hear faint murmurs of its joy, he wished that he was there. One morning when he awoke it struck him that the opposite shore was unusually nigh, and so low was the tide that he fancied he might easily ford it, or swim across. And so he hastened forth. First over the dry shingle, then over the sad and solid sand from which, with scarce a ripple, the sea had smoothly folded down, he hurried on till he reached the damper strand, where streams of laggard water still were trickling, and then was astonished at his own delusion; for it was still a mighty gulf, and even whilst he gazed the tide was rising. But another time he tried another plan. To the right of his dwelling the line of coast stretched away in a succession of cliffs and headlands, till the view was bounded by a lofty promontory which seemed to touch the farther side. To this promontory he resolved to take a pilgrimage, in the hope that it would transport him to the long-sought realm. The road was often a steep clamber, and for many an hour the headland seemed only to flee away. But after surmounting many a slope and swell, at last he reached it. With eager steps he ran along the ridge, half hoping that it was the isthmus which would bear him to the blessed isle. Ah, no! He has reached its extremest verge, and here is that inexorable ocean still weltering at its base. Baffled in this last hope, and faint with his ineffectual toil, he flung himself on the stones and wept. But, by-and-by, he noticed off the shore a little boat with whose appearance he was quite familiar. It used to ride at anchor opposite his own abode, and had done so for ever so long; but, like his neighbors, he had got so used to it that it never drew his notice. Now, however, seeing it there, he looked at it, and as he looked it neared him. It came close up to the rocks where he was seated. It was a beautiful boat with snowy sails and golden prow, and a red cross was its waving pennon. There was one on board, and only one. His raiment was white and glistening, and his features betokened whence he came. "Son of man," he said, "why weepest thou?" "Because I cannot reach the blessed Isle." "Canst thou trust thyself with me?" the stranger asked. The poor wayfarer looked at the little skiff leaping lightly on the waves, and won dered, till he looked again at the pilot's kind and assuring countenance, and then he said, "I can." And no sooner had he stepped on board than, swift as a sunbeam, it bore him to the land of light; and, with many a welcome from the pilot's friends, he found himself among its happy citizens, clothed in their bright raiment, and free to all their privileges as now a subject of their King.

The happy isle is peace with God,—that position which man occupied whilst innocent. The dreary land is that state of alienation and misery into which fallen man is banished. The little skiff denotes the only means by which the sinner may pass from nature's alienation over into the peace of God. It is a means not of the sinners devising, but of God's providing. It is the ATONEMENT, and He who so kindly invites sinner's to avail themselves of it is the Lord Jesus Himself.

I may suppose the case of a hearer who longs for acceptance with God. At present you feel like an exile looking at a distant Eden with a gulf between. You feel that between you and God's favor there rolls a tide of trespasses and sins which all your efforts cannot get over. Sometimes, like the poor outcast on that bright morning, you have flattered yourself that the separating interval had narrowed, and if all went favorably you did not despair of finding yourself ere long in the climes of ascertained salvation. But even then, like a broad and powerful tide, the current of worldliness set in again, and the interval betwixt God and your own soul again grew vast as ever; or, the dark stream of guilt began once more to roar and deepen. Therefore, ceasing to hope that your soul's salvation would come about spontaneously, you set to work on purpose to achieve it. Like one who would bridge across the mighty channel; or rather, like one who sets out on pilgrimage to yon inviting promontory,—you go about to establish a righteousness of your own. You resolve to read so many chapters and to pray so many times a-day. You determine that you will henceforth never more be angry, nor deceitful, nor neglectful of your trust. You try to think holy thoughts and make your own mind spiritual. And in this way you hope to go on by degrees till you are really good,—so good that you may be at last forgiven. But how far must the traveller march round the coast of Europe before he arrives in Britain? And how many things must the sinner do in a state of nature before he finds himself in a state of grace? They that are in the flesh cannot please God, and instead of being good in order to be forgiven, you had need to be forgiven as the first movement towards becoming good. The separating gulf is too deep for the tallest specimen of human virtue to ford, and too wide for the sincerest repentance or the most faultless morality to bridge over; and were you confronting the realities of the case you would find that Christless painstaking is only a pilgrimage along a sea-girt promontory. Peace with God is not a boon which it requires good deeds to purchase or prayers to ensure; but peace with God is a gift from God, already come from heaven and awaiting your acceptance. And, just as the vexed wanderer lifted up his eyes, and in the boat, with its benignant pilot, recognized the little skiff which had so long hovered unheeded near his own abode; so, were the Spirit of God to make you earnest now,—were He convincing you of sin or of the futility of your own exertions, you would see your salvation in some thrice-told tale,—some text with which you have been familiar long ago. "Eternal life is the gift of God." "God hath given to us eternal life, and this life is in his Son." "To as many as received Him Jesus gave power to become the sons of God, even to them that believe on his name." "The Son of man must be lifted up, that whosoever believeth in Him may not perish, but have eternal life." "Look unto me and be ye saved all the ends of the earth." Like some dim object anchored near your dwelling, texts like these are associated with your earliest memory. These texts are gospels. Any one of them is such 'a faithful saying," that fully realized and implicitly credited it would carry your soul to heaven. Any one of them is an ark of salvation with none less than the Friend of sinners in it; and you have only to be persuaded of its good-will and its trustworthiness, so as to transfer your immortal interests to the Saviour's keeping, and you will soon discover that TRUST IN CHRIST IS PEACE WITH GOD.

A justifying righteousness is not a privilege which you buy, but a present which you receive. It is not a result which you accomplish, nor a reward which you earn, but it is a gratuity which you accept. It is the "gift of righteousness,"—a gift promiscuous to sinners of our race,—a gift as wide as the human "whosoever;" a gift outstanding which was within the reach of your earliest intelligence had you been so disposed, and which is not yet withdrawn,—a gift which it needs neither prayer to bring nearer nor a price before or after to make surer, but which it only needs your open hand, your open heart to make your personal possession;—not a bargain, but a boon; not an achievement, but an acquiescence; the gift of righteousness;—the righteousness of God which seeks, not that we deserve it, but that we "submit" to it. Being justified freely by his grace through the redemption that is in Christ, God's righteousness is declared through the remission of sins that are past. And being justified by faith we have peace with God, through our Lord Jesus Christ. Thanks be to God for his unspeakable gift!

Thus is it that the right relation between God and the sinner is established; a relation which borrows all its security and blessedness from the sinner's substitute, God's own Son. Our redemption is in Christ, and it is in the Beloved that we are accepted. Our safety is all in the Saviour whom we trust. He is our peace. Immanuel is the door. It is by Him that we enter into the fold and become the sheep of his Father.

And when once the right relation is brought about, the right affection must follow. It could not come before. It did not come whilst the portion of goods held out, and amidst his riotous living the prodigal was jeering at the decorum and dulness of his Father's house. And it did not come when the penniless outcast was envying the swine, and yet was too proud to go home. And it did not come when crushed and crest-fallen the runaway bent his steps towards the forsaken threshold, and all his thought was how to propitiate an angry father, and how, if he could only get a hearing, he might get leave to labor for his food, and so, from an out-door menial, gradually work his way back to the hearth and the family board. But when, instead of an angry and upbraiding stranger, he found a yearning parent; and, instead of the menial's garb, saw himself invested in the honored guest's best robe; and instead of the meanest hireling's place, was installed at a sumptuous festival; when he saw these eyes suffused with all the love of delighted fatherhood, and still felt on his neck where that father's tears had fallen,—then it came—the filial affection came; the long dormant instinct of sonship revived, and the love of a fervent gratitude mingled,—so that in all the Holy Land the fullest heart that night was the restored and forgiven prodigal.

And even so, that filial emotion which here

and throughout the Old Testament, is often called "fear;" that blended emotion of reverence, trust, and affection, can only arise where the spirit of sonship reciprocates God's revealed aspect of compassionate and forthgoing fatherliness. It matters little whether we call the affection fear, or, with the first and great commandment, call it love. In that fear which realizes God's fatherliness, there cannot be terror; and in the love which recollects that its father is God there cannot be petulant boldness.

Fear God, therefore, for this is the great duty of man. To love Him with all the heart and soul and strength and mind, is the first and great commandment; and till once Jehovah is supreme, an orderly and respectable life is only rebellion without violence, and even benevolence without godliness is only a beautiful impiety.

LECTURE XXI.

Green Pastures.

"Let us hear the conclusion of the whole matter: Fear God, and keep his commandments: for this is the whole of man."—ECCLES. XII. 13.

"THIS is life eternal, to know Thee, the only true God, and Jesus Christ whom thou hast sent." To get this knowledge is to enter into blessedness. Reconciliation to God is like entering the gate of a beautiful avenue, which conducts to a splendid mansion. But that avenue is long, and in some places it skirts the edge of dangerous cliffs; and therefore, to save the traveller from falling over and being dashed to pieces, it is fenced all the way by a quick-set hedge. That hedge is the commandments. They are planted there that we may do ourselves no harm. But, like a fence of the fragrant brier, they regale the pilgrim who keeps the path, and they only hurt him when he tries to break through. Temperance, justice, truthfulness; purity of speech and behavior; obedience to parents; mutual affection; sanctification of the Sabbath; the reverent worship of God;—all these are righteous requirements, and in keeping them there is a great reward. Happy he who only knows the precept in the perfume which it sheds, and who, never having kicked against the pricks, has never proved the sharpness of its thorns!

In its happy influence, religion, or a filial compliance with the will of God, includes "the whole of man." It is self-contained felicity.

A new heart itself is happiness. The rain as it falls from the firmament is never poisonous; but by the time it filters through strata filled with lead or copper, it may become so pernicious that whosoever drinks of the water dies. The juice of the grape, as it flows from the fermenting vat, is generous wine; but if the wine-skin which receives it is old and musty, or if it be poured into a jar of acidulous pottery, it soon grows sour and vapid. Gifts as they come from God are always good and perfect; but by the time that they have distilled through our murmuring spirits, they assume a different character. From the way he speaks of them, you would fancy that the worldling's joy had all been drawn from Marah; or that, however carefully he had covered over his own cistern, the star Wormwood had dropped into it, and changed the whole to a deadly bitter. The truth is, his mind is its own Marah, and his morose and murmuring nature is the wormwood which renders acrid to the taste the mercies of God. But Christianity is a new creation. The Gospel renovates the soul; and, putting a right spirit in the man, it makes him a blessed being by making him a RIGHT RECIPIENT. When the water is as clear as was the well of Bethlehem; or when the wine flows as rich as the vintage of Lebanon,—all that is needful is a pitcher of crystal or a goblet of silver, which by infusing no new element, will preserve its freshness and purity. And when gifts are so good as the

Gospel and the promises;—so good as our kindred and friends;—so good as the flowers of the field and the breath of the new summer,—it only needs an honest heart which takes them as they come, and which tastes unaltered the goodness of God that is in them. This is what the worldling wants; this new heart is what the God and Father of our Lord Jesus offers to you, to me.

The very faculty of joy is the gift of the Holy Ghost. There is a canker in the heart of man which hinders happiness even when the materials are most abundant; and it is mournful to observe how little gladness is felt even when corn and wine most abound. In the midst of affluence still anxious, the munificence of the Creator cannot give contentment to worldlings and worldly professors; but whilst the green pastures re-echo their grumblings, they may see their peevish faces reflected in those quiet waters to which their kind Shepherd has led them. It needs more than good and perfect gifts to awaken melody and praise: and unless the Spirit of God made it a thankful heart, the providence of God cannot make it a happy existence. But when the Comforter is come, he gives a new heart, and creates a right spirit. He heals the canker of the churl and sweetens the bitterness of the misanthrope; and, by imparting the faculty of joy, he has often exalted life into a jubilee and made a very humble dwelling ring with hallelujahs. Ever since it was broken at the fall, the heart of man is a cracked pitcher from which happiness runs out with amazing rapidity; and the finer the fluid—the more subtle the element of joy—the faster does it trickle through; and often it is not till the last drop is oozing,—it is not till the latest film is regretfully vanishing, that the soul knows it ought to have been happy, and is sorry for not knowing it sooner.* Far otherwise is it with the Christian's pleasures. He who has made him a new creature, has given him a new capacity of receiving

* "The sweetness that pleasure has in it
Is always so slow to come forth,
That seldom, alas, till the minute
It dies, do we know half its worth."
Moore's Melodies.

and retaining joy. The new heart does not leak; at least, there is one gladness there which will abide to all eternity, and which, even when it has for a season disappeared, needs nothing but the jolts of sorrow to shake it up again in all its sparkling zest and fragrant exhilaration. The soul into which God has put the gladness can never be empty of all joy; for the "joy of salvation" heals the broken heart, and so long as itself remains it makes it possible for other joys to stay.

A devout disposition is happiness. It is happiness, whether outward things go well or ill. A comfortable home, fond kindred, health, a successful calling, are sweet mercies when you accept them direct from God,—thus rendering dearer to yourself, at once the giver and the gifts. But these mercies may, one by one, withdraw. Lover and friend may be put far from you, and your acquaintance may vanish into secret; your house may dilapidate; your industrious efforts may be defeated; and your prosperous state may be exchanged for penury. But "although the fig-tree shall not blossom, neither shall fruit be in the vines; the labor of the olive shall fail, and the fields shall yield no meat; the flock shall be cut off from the fold, and there shall be no herds in the stalls; yet you will rejoice in the Lord, and will joy in the God of your salvation." With shattered constitution you may find yourself confined to your couch or your chamber, and in pain and depression you may miss that presence which would have been a "sunshine in this shady place." But lonely and languid you can say, "Whom have I in heaven but thee? and there is none upon earth that I desire beside thee. My flesh and my heart faileth; but God is the strength of my heart, and my portion forever." Public affairs may take a sombre turn, and in the growth of pauperism, or in the wider gulf that sunders the classes, there may be prognostics of uproar and anarchy; or in one of those fits of infatuation which occasionally seize society, you may stand aghast at educated men flinging away their human rights and their reason, and surrendering to a grim superstition which puts out their eyes and binds them in the fetters of Babylon;* or under the spurring hoof of some colossal despotism, you may hear human hearts crushing, as the sea-weed crackles under the school-boy's wanton heel, and in vain sympathy you may burst your own; or, as in volcanic reaction, pent-up indignation at last explodes, and thrones and altars are hurled through mid-heaven, whilst civilization is overwhelmed beneath the fiery tide, like grass under lava, and as it spirts into the air, the gory geyser tells where the earth has opened her mouth, and swallowed alive a weltering multitude;—in moments like these, when the most hopeful philanthrophy is paralyzed, and "men's hearts fail them for fear," the believer can sing, "God is our refuge and strength, a very present help in trouble. Therefore will not we fear, though the earth be removed, and the mountains be carried into the midst of the sea:" and beyond all the crash and the turmoil, his purer ear can catch the cadence of heavenly harpers, and through all the smoke

* 2 Kings xxv. 7.

of burning mountains quenched in boiling seas, his penetrating eye can glimpse the tokens of a bright Epiphany: and from the reeling soil, he lifts up his head, knowing that redemption draweth nigh. Oh brethren! in those solemn conjunctures which prefigure final judgment; in those awful conflicts where man appears not so much the combatant as the arena; in those Armageddons where man cannot look to man, for the contending powers are Jehovah and Apollyon,—how blessed to have a friend in Omnipotence, and a citadel within the tabernacle of the Most High!

A benevolent disposition is happiness. The first and great commandment is, "Thou shalt love the Lord thy God with all thy soul; and the second is like unto it, Thou shalt love thy neighbor as thyself." To keep these two commandments is the whole of man. The two feelings are very different. It is with an adorning complacency that you love the ever-blessed, desiring that his glory should be advanced, and that his will should be the mind of the universe. It is with an affectionate good-will that you love your fellow-creatures, desiring that they should be happy in loyalty to God. The one love is simply outgoing; the other ascends. The one is kindness; the other is full of worship. The one is filial devotion; the other is paternal fondness.

When a rose-bud is formed, if the soil is soft and the sky is genial, it is not long before it bursts; for the life within is so abundant that it can no longer contain it all,—but in blossomed brightness and swimming fragrance it must needs let forth its joy, and gladden all the air. And if, when thus ripe, it refused to expand, it would quickly rot at heart, and die. And Christian charity is just piety with its petals fully spread, developing itself, and making it a happier world. The religion which fancies that it loves God, when it never evinces love to its brother, is not piety but a poor mildewed theology,—a dogma with a worm in its heart.

Benevolence is blessedness. It is God's life in the soul, diffusing in kind emotions, and good offices, and friendly intercessions; but, unlike other expenditures, the more it is diffused, the more that life increases of which it is the sign, and to abound in love one towards another, is to abound in hope towards God.

This was Solomon's calamity. In his auspicious outset he lived for others. To make Jehovah's temple exceedingly magnificent and to see his people prosperous, were the great desires of his forthgoing patriotism and piety. But in a mysterious moment he was forsaken by God's Spirit. To his introverted egotism his own interest became more urgent than all the universe, and the saint and the patriot became a selfist. The lily crept back into its bulb. It said, I am myself the summer. Yon sun shines, because I am to be seen. This air is balm, because it encircles me. I will go down into myself, and what a self-contained Eden it will be when all my glory is reserved for Solomon! And down it went; but though its disappearance left less of summer in the world, nothing but winter was found below. And it was not till he took another thought, and resolved once more to keep these two commands that aught of his old glory came again.

Benevolence is blessedness; and if the present age is happier than some that have gone before it, a chief reason is because its heart is kinder. Doubtless, the amount of material comfort is amazingly increased; but this is not enough. Man is not a dormouse; and however warmly he lines his nest, and however snug the pose of orbicular self-complacency into which he rolls himself, he cannot become his own all-in-all. Material comforts multiply; but these alone have not made it a happier age. It is happier because it is kinder. We would rather convert the Turks than kill them. We would rather see France virtuous and God-fearing, than see it subject to Britain. We would rather teach the Jews the Gospel than torture from them their money hoards. This is the age which wishes well to the slave, and has paid a great price for his freedom. This is the age whieh wishes well to the Heathen, and is paying, if not a great price, yet a greater than was ever paid before, for his Christian civilization. This is the age which wishes well to the poor and the outcast, and which is taking great pains to enlighten his mind and exalt his condition. God forbid that we should boast. Human nature is the same now as ever; but if the Father of mercies has somewhat softened the spirit of this age, let us not forget to bless his holy name. We think he has. We think on the whole that the world is happier, because of late the Lord has made it somewhat kinder. And its happiness will advance in proportion as it learns to realize that object of the advent,—"on earth peace; good-will towards men."

Malevolence is misery. It is the mind of Satan. He is the great enemy,—an outcast from all joy, and an opponent of all goodness and all blessedness. His mind is enmity against God; enmity against angels fallen and unfallen; enmity against man both redeemed and reprobate; and, because thus hateful and hating, utterly unhappy. And the carnal mind is so far Satanic because it is enmity against God; just as the misanthrope is so far

Satanic because he is enmity against his fellows. On the other hand, benevolence is happiness. It is the mind of God, whose tender mercies are over all his works, and who joys in the joy of his creation. And hence it comes to pass that some who have never tasted the full blessedness of piety, have enjoyed many sweet satisfactions in the exercise of benevolence. "Oh world," says the Emperor Antoninus, "all things are suitable to me which are suitable to thee. Nothing is too early or too late for me which is seasonable for thee. All is fruit to me which thy seasons bring forth. Shall any man say, O beloved city of Cecrops! and wilt not thou say, O beloved city of God." "And you, my brothers," exclaimed the German Richter, after he had spent some years in severely satirizing men and manners: seized with a sudden compunction, or rather yielding to a genial visitation, "And you, my brothers, I will love you more. I will create for you more joy. I will no longer turn my comic powers to torment you; but antasy and wit shall be united to find consolation and cheerfulness for the most limited of life's relations."* He kept his word. Moroseness and moodiness fled away, and from that period onward, there are few lives not saintly, on which care's shadow sits more lightly. But if there be such a solace in mere benevolence; if there be such a Divine delightsomeness in drying tears and diffusing happiness; if some have passed a very pleasant life who were only kind-hearted without being Christian;—how incomparably more blessed are those who unite the two,—whose brotherly kindness is the fruit of faith, and whose charity is a devout benevolence! the John who, basking in the rays of uncreated love, returns into the midst of our mortality with a glow which ever since has raised the temperature of time! the Paul who, catching the spirit of his Master, in the daily medium through which heaven's kindness finds its way to the heart of our humanity, and whose very soul, like a libation on a sacrifice, goes up a sweet savor to God, and leaves on earth a grateful memory!

* Richter's Autobiography, vol. ii. 196.

Brethren, seek loving thoughts of God. Pray for them. Cherish them. Strive to realize his true character. Look not at the distortions drawn by the lurid fancy of superstition; look not at the dark pictures sketched by your own guilty conscience. But look at the Bible revelation. Look at Immanuel. Behold the brightness of the Father's glory—behold the word incarnate, full of grace and truth. Surrender to the manifestation. Let your aspect towards Jehovah be the reciprocal of his aspect towards you. Look towards Jesus, and with the pleasant countenance wherewith he views his beloved Son, he will behold you, oh looking transgressor! I should rather say, oh justified believer! And by praise, and by bright obedience, and cheerful trust, seek to augment your love to your heavenly Father. When happy thoughts come into your mind, let the thought of God come with them; and when you go into beautiful or attractive scenes, let the reconciled Presence go with you; till at last earth is suffused with heaven, and with the immortal morning spread upon the mountains death is done away and the oak valley superseded.

And seek, as a fruit of the Spirit, love. As a Christian principle cultivate a broad benevolence, and by-and-by you will come to feel it as a delightful and spontaneous instinct. Having, in virtue of your redeemed relation, "a covenant with the beasts of the field and with the creeping things of the ground," you will come to share the creature-ward complacency of that kind Creator whose tender mercies are over all his works, and perhaps may realize the description with which you have sometimes been charmed:—

> "In the silence of his face I read
> His overflowing spirit. Birds and beasts,
> And the mute fish that glances in the stream,
> And harmless reptile coiling in the sun,
> And gorgeous insect moving in the air,
> The fowl domestic, and the household dog—
> In his capacious mind he loved them all.
> Rich in love
> And sweet humanity, he was himself,
> To the degree that he desired, beloved."*

But even this creature-ward kindliness will

* Wordsworth's "Excursion," book 2.

profit you little unless it be combined with that sublime love towards your immortal fellows which constitutes Christian charity. Love man as man. Fallen and sinful, he is still your brother. Pity the sinner even whilst you abhor the sin; and, in order to deepen and purify your compassion, let it assume a practical form. Ask yourself, what am I doing to make it a holier and so a happier world? And if you find that you are doing nothing in this Divine direction, be not surprised that there is still a crook in your lot and a discomfort in your spirit. Existence will only run smooth when you learn to be a fellow-worker with God. And love the believing brethren. Rejoice in their increase. Rejoice in their prosperity. Glorify the grace of God in them, and be so heartily solicitous for their progress and improvement as really to help them forward. And loving without dissimulation, you will soon find yourself the centre of much affection in return, and whatever joy you diffuse you will find it all returning with increase into your own bosom.

BOOKS

PUBLISHED BY

ROBERT CARTER & BROTHERS,

285 BROADWAY, NEW-YORK.

ABEEL'S (Rev. David) Life. By his Nephew. 18mo,.... $ 50
ABERCROMBIE'S Contest and The Armour. 32mo, gilt, 25
ADAM'S Three Divine Sisters—Faith, Hope and Charity,... 60
ADVICE TO A YOUNG CHRISTIAN. 18mo,....... 30
ALLEINE'S Gospel Promises. 18mo,.................... 30
——— Life and Letters. 12mo,........................... 60
ALEXANDER'S Counsels to the Young. 32mo, gilt...... 25
ANCIENT HISTORY of the Egyptians, Assyrians, &c., 4 vols.,.. 2 00
ANDERSON'S Annals of the English Bible. 8vo,........ 1 75
——— Family Book. 12mo,................................ 75
AUSTRALIA, the Loss of the Brig, by Fire. 18mo,...... 25
BAGSTER—The Authenticity and Inspiration of the Bible, 60
BAXTER'S Saint's Rest. Large type. 12mo,............ 60
— — Call to the Unconverted. 18mo,..................... 30
——— Choice Works. 12mo,................................ 60
BIBLE EXPOSITOR. Illustrated. 18mo,.............. 50
BICKERSTETH'S Treatise on Prayer. 18mo,........... 40
——— Treatise on the Lord's Supper. 18mo,.............. 30
BLOSSOMS OF CHILDHOOD. By the author of the "Broken Bud." 16mo,................................ .
BLUNT'S Undesigned Coincidences, and Paley's Horæ Paulinæ. In one volume 8vo,........................... 2 00
BOGATZKY'S Golden Treasury. 24mo, gilt,............. 50

BONAR'S (Rev. Horatius) Night of Weeping,............ 30
—— Morning of Joy, a sequel to the above,............... 40
—— Story of Grace,.................................... 30
—— Truth and Error. 18mo,............................ 40
BONAR'S (Rev. Andrew) Commentary on Leviticus. 8vo, 1 50
BONNET'S Family of Bethany. 18mo,.................. 40
—— Meditations on the Lord's Prayer. 18mo,............ 40
BOOTH'S Reign of Grace. 12mo,........................ 75
BORROW'S Bible and Gipsies of Spain. 8vo, cloth. New Edition,.. 1 00
BOSTON'S Four-fold State. 18mo,...................... 50
—— Crook in the Lot. 18mo,........................... 30
BROKEN BUD; or, the Reminiscences of a Bereaved Mother. 16mo,.. 75
BROWN'S (Rev. John, D.D.) Exposition of First Peter. 8vo, 2 50
—— On the Sayings and Discourses of Christ,............
BROWN'S Explication of the Assembly's Catechism. 12mo, 60
BROWN (Rev. David) on the Second Advent. 12mo,..... 1 25
BRIDGES on the Christian Ministry. 8vo,................ 1 50
—— on the Proverbs. 8vo,............................. 2 00
—— on the CXIX. Psalm. New edition. 8vo,............ 1 00
—— Memoir of Mary Jane Graham. 8vo,................ 1 00
—— Works. 3 vols. 8vo, containing the above,.......... 5 00
BROWN'S Concordance. New and neat edition. 24mo,... 20
Do. Gilt edge,....................... 30
BUCHANAN'S Comfort in Affliction. 18mo,.............. 40
—— On the Holy Spirit. 18mo. Second edition,......... 50
BUNBURY'S Glory, Glory, Glory, and other Narratives,... 25
BUTLER'S (Bishop) Complete Works. 8vo,............. 1 50
—— Sermons, alone. 8vo,.............................. 1 00
—— Analogy, alone. 8vo,.............................. 75
—— and Wilson's Analogy. 8vo,........................ 1 25
BUNYAN'S Pilgrim's Progress, fine edition, large type. 12mo, 1 00
Do. Gilt,........................ 1 50
Do. 18mo, close type,........... 50
—— Jerusalem Sinner Saved. 18mo,................. .. 50
—— Greatness of the Soul. 18mo,...................... 50
BURN'S (John) Christian Fragments. 18mo,.............. 40
BURNS' (Rev. Jabez) Parables and Miracles of Christ. 12mo, 75
CALVIN—The Life and Times of John Calvin, the Great Reformer. By Paul Henry, D.D. 2 vols. 8vo, Portrait,....... 3 00
CAMERON'S (Mrs.) Farmer's Daughter. 18mo,......... 30

CATECHISMS—The Assembly's Catechism. Per hundred, 1 25
—— with Proofs,.. 3 00
—— Brown's Short Catechism. Per hundred,............ 1 25
—— Brown on the Assembly's Catechism. 18mo,....... 10
CECIL'S WORKS. 3 vols. 12mo, with Portrait,.......... 3 00
—— Sermons, separate,................................. 1 00
—— Miscellanies and Remains, separate,................. 1 00
—— Original Thoughts, separate,......................... 1 00
—— (Catharine) Memoir of Mrs. Hawks, with Portrait. 1 00
CHARNOCK'S Choice Works,.......................... 60
CHALMERS' Sermons. 2 vols. 8vo. With a fine Portrait, 3 00
—— Lectures on Romans. 8vo. " " 1 50
—— Miscellanies. 8vo. " " 1 50
—— Select Works; comprising the above. 4 vols. 8vo,... 6 00
—— Evidences of Christian Revelation. 2 vols.,.......... 1 25
—— Natural Theology. 2 vols.,............................ 1 25
—— Moral Philosophy,.................................... 60
—— Commercial Discourses,............................... 60
—— Astronomical Discourses,............................. 60
CHEEVER'S Lectures on the Pilgrim's Progress. Illustrated. 12mo,... 1 00
CHRISTIAN RETIREMENT. 12mo,................ 75
—— **EXPERIENCE.** By the same Author. 12mo,.... 75
CLARK'S (Rev. John A.,) Walk about Zion. 12mo,...... 75
—— Pastor's Testimony,................................. 75
—— Awake, Thou Sleeper,............................... 75
—— Young Disciple,...................................... 88
—— Gathered Fragments,................................. 1 00
CLARKE'S Daily Scripture Promises. 32mo, gilt,........ 30
COLQUHOUN'S (Lady) World's Religion. New ed., 16mo, 50
COMMANDMENT WITH PROMISE. By the Author of "The Week," &c. Illustrated by Howland. 16mo,.... 75
Do. do. do. gilt, 1 00
COWPER.—The Works of William Cowper; comprising his Life, Letters and Poems, now first collected by the introduction of Cowper's Private Correspondence. Edited by the Rev. T. S. Grimshaw. With numerous illustrations on steel, and a fine Portrait by Ritchie. 1 vol. royal 8vo,.. 3 00
Do. do. cloth, extra gilt, 4 00
Do. do. morocco extra, 5 00
—— Poetical Works, complete, separate. 2 vols. 16mo. Illustrated,.. 1 50
Do. do. do. gilt, 2 00

CUMMING'S (Rev. John, D.D.) Message from God. 18mo, 30
—— Christ Receiving Sinners,........................ 30
CUNNINGHAM'S World without Souls. 18mo,......... 30
CUYLER'S (Rev. T. L.) Stray Arrows,.................... 30
DALE (Rev. Thomas)—The Golden Psalm. 16mo,........ 60
DAVIES' Sermons. 3 vols. 12mo,........................ 2 00
DAVIDSON'S (Dr.) Connexions. New edition. 8vo,..... 1 50
Do. do. 3 vols. 12mo,.......... 1 50
DAVID'S PSALMS, in metre. Large type. 12mo, emb. 75
Do. do. gilt edge, 1 00
Do. do. Turkey morocco, 2 00
Do. 18mo, good type, plain sheep,................ 38
Do. 48mo, very neat pocket edition, sheep,.......... 20
Do. " " " morocco,....... 25
Do. " " " gilt edge,....... 31
Do. " " " tucks,.......... 50
Do. with Brown's Notes. 18mo,.................... 50
Do. " " morocco gilt,...... 1 00
D'AUBIGNE'S History of the Reformation. *Carefully Revised*, with various additions not hitherto published. 4 vols. in two. 12mo, cloth,.............................. 1 50
Do. do. 8vo, complete in 1 vol., 1 00
—— Life of Cromwell the Protector. 12mo,.............. 50
—— Germany, England, and Scotland. 12mo,............ 75
—— Luther and Calvin. 18mo,......................... 25
—— The Authority of God the true Barrier against Infidel and Romish Aggression,.............................. 75
DICK'S (John, D.D.) Lectures on Theology. Fine edition, with Portrait. 2 vols. in one. Cloth,..................... 2 50
Do. do. sheep, 3 00
Do. do. in 2 vols., cloth, 3 00
—— Lectures on Acts. 8vo,.............................. 1 50
DICKINSON'S (Rev. R. W.) Scenes from Sacred History, 1 00
—— Responses from the Sacred Oracles,................ 1 00
DODDRIDGE'S Rise and Progress. 18mo,............... 40
—— Life of Colonel Gardiner. 18mo,.................... 30
DUNCAN'S Sacred Philosophy of the Seasons. 4 vols.,... 3 00
—— Life. By his Son. With Portrait. 12mo,........... 75
—— Tales of the Scottish Peasantry. 18mo. Illustrated,.. 50
—— Cottage Fireside. 18mo,.......................... 40
—— (Mrs.) Life of Mary Lundie Duncan. 16mo,......... 75
—— —— Life of George A. Lundie. 18mo,............ 50

DUNCANS (Mrs.) Memoir of George B. Phillips. 18mo,.. 25
—— —— Children of the Manse,........................ 1 00
Do. do. gilt,.................... 1 25
—— (Mary Lundie) Rhymes for my Children. Illustrated, 25
EDWARDS' (Jonathan D.D.) Discourses on Christian Love, never before published. 12mo,........................
ERSKINE'S Gospel Sonnets. 18mo. Portrait,........... 50
ENGLISH PULPIT. 8vo,............................ 1 50
EVIDENCES OF CHRISTIANITY. A Course of Lectures delivered before the University of Virginia. 8vo,...
FAMILY WORSHIP. A series of Prayers for every Morning and Evening throughout the year, adapted to Domestic Worship. By one hundred and eighty clergymen of Scotland. 8vo,......................................
Do. do. do. gilt,
Do. do. do. morocco,
FERGUSON'S Roman Republic. 8vo,.................. 1 50
FISK'S Memorial of the Holy Land. With steel plates,.... 1 00
FLEURY'S Life of David. 12mo,...................... 60
FOSTER'S Essays on Decision of Character, &c. Large type, 75
Do. do. close type, 18mo, 50
—— Essay on the Evils of Popular Ignorance. 12mo,..... 75
FORD'S Decapolis. 18mo,.............................. 25
FOX—Memoir of the Rev. Henry Watson Fox, Missionary to the Teloogoos. Illustrated. 12mo,...................... 1 00
FRY (Caroline)—The Listener. 2 vols. in one. New illustrated edition. 16mo,.. .... 1 00
—— Christ on Law. 12mo,............ 60
—— Sabbath Musings. 18mo,.......................... 40
—— The Scripture Reader's Guide. 18mo,.............. 30
—— Christ our Example, and Autobiography. 16mo,.....
GEOLOGICAL COSMOGNY.. By a Layman. 18mo,.. 30
GOD IN THE STORM. 18mo,...................... . 25
GRAHAM'S Test of Truth. 18mo,...................... 30
GREEN—The Life of the Rev. Ashbel Green, D.D. 8vo,... 2 00
GRIFFITH'S Live while you Live. 18mo,............... 30
HALDANE'S Exposition of Romans. 8vo,.... .... 2 50
HALL'S (Bishop) Select Works. 16mo,.................. 75
HAMILTON'S (Rev. James D.D.) Life in Earnest. 18mo, 30
—— Mount of Olives. 18mo,............................ 30
—— Harp on the Willows. 18mo,....................... 30
—— Thankfulness. 18mo,.............................. 30

HAMILTON'S Life of Hall. 24mo, gilt,.................. 30
——— Happy Home. Illustrated. 18mo,............... ... 50
——— Life of Lady Colquhoun. 16mo,........ 75
Do. do. " gilt,................. 1 00
——— The Royal Preacher; or, Lectures on Ecclesiastes. Portrait. 16mo,.. 85
Do. do. do. gilt, 1 25
HAWKER'S Poor Man's Morning Portion. 12mo,........ 60
Do. do. Evening Portion. " 60
——— Zion's Pilgrim. 18mo,............................ 30
HERVEY'S Meditations. 18mo,........................ 40
HETHERINGTON'S History of the Church of Scotland, 1 50
HENRY'S (Matth.) Method for Prayer,.................. 40
——— Communicant's Companion. 18mo,................. 40
——— Daily Communion with God. " 30
——— Pleasantness of a Religious Life. 24mo, gilt,........ 30
——— Choice Works. 12mo,.... 60
HENRY, Philip, Life of. 18mo,......................... 50
HEWITSON—Memoir of the Rev. W. H. Hewitson, Free Church Minister at Dirleton, Scotland, with Portrait. 12mo, 85
Do. do. do. gilt, 1 25
HILL'S (George) Lectures on Divinity. 8vo,.............. 2 00
——— (Rowland) Life. By Sidney. 12mo,................ 75
HISTORY OF THE PURITANS IN ENGLAND, AND THE PILGRIM FATHERS. By Stowell and Wilson. 12mo,....................................... 1 00
HISTORY OF THE REFORMATION IN EUROPE. 40
HOUSMAN'S Life and Remains. 12mo,................ 75
HORNE'S Introduction. 2 vols. royal 8vo, half cloth,..... 3 50
Do. do. 1 vol. sheep,.. .... 4 00
Do. do. 2 vols. cloth,.................... 4 00
Do. do. 2 vols, library style,............. 5 00
——— (Bishop,) Commentary on the Book of Psalms,......... 1 50
HOWELL'S LIFE—Perfect Peace. 18mo,............... 30
HOWE'S Redeemer's Tears, and other Essays. 18mo,...... 50
HOWARD, (John,) or the Prison World of Europe. 12mo,. 1 00
HOOKER, (Rev. H.,) The Uses of Adversity. 18mo,...... 30
——— Philosophy of Unbelief,........................... 75
HUSS, (John,) Life of. Translated from the German,...... 25
INFANT'S PROGRESS. By the Author of "Little Henry and his Bearer." Illustrated 16mo,.................. 75
Do. do. " gilt,... .... 1 00

Edward Irving came to London in 1822, and James Hamilton in 1841. Dr. Hamilton was another man than his predecessor, yet with an individuality of his own as marked; exquisitely unique, richly touched with humour and pathos, not at all daring, more balanced, though milder, temperament, and larger know[illegible]ledge of varied themes; therefore, calmer, wh[illegible] not at all so lofty or impassioned as Ir[illegible]. But Hamilton also had in common with Ir[illegible], his one best gift of grace and of a gracious[illegible] to use his own word, winsome—holy li[illegible] [illegible], too, belongs, if not to the heroes, yet t[illegible] [illegible]nts of all times; and few men were more[illegible] [illegible]ous than he was of the tendencies of his own period. Coming back to its Divine origin and work in the world, this period is marked by the way in which the Church strove to assert and embody them. This took three directions. The first may be called the upward. Therein the Church rose to a definite and passionate conviction of its dependence on God, and none else. From this sprang three distinct movements. First, that of the Voluntary controversy, with its principle of the correlation of two independent powers—the Church and the State—and of these as working best when each works independently. The second was the Disruption controversy, which asserted that whatever the relation of the Church and the State it should not by a hair's-breadth touch the independent life and inalienable functions of the Church. Hence the greatest modern deed of faith which has added a new demonstration to the Divine origin and independence of Christianity breathed a higher temper in all Churches, and has as its monument the Free Church of Scotland. That noble struggle has also, after many fortunes, brought us together, through its sundering of old ties, into a new and happy united Church. But, again, and thirdly, there was the beginning of the Oxford Tractarian movement, asserting the claims of an independence in the Church, true in its deepest principle, but entangled with and raising into power many old and dangerous errors, especially that Popish extreme of the Church in which every other human society is treated as a blind slave, and not as a free and intelligent ally of the spiritual power. The second great movement taking an inward direction—that for union in the Church rising out of the quickened sense of its independence—threw into consciousness and activity its essential harmony within itself. Hence began the period of aiming at closer, more declared union in many forms. James Hamilton, following his great master, Thomas Chalmers—one of the greatest heroes of modern times, near whose centenary year we meet—as well as his own generous spirit, was the very apostle of union; and let us not forget that to none of the dead do we owe our gathering to-night as a united Church more than to James Hamilton.

1879,

www.ingramcontent.com/pod-product-compliance
Lightning Source LLC
LaVergne TN
LVHW020119110826
845151LV00001B/210

* 9 7 8 1 4 2 5 5 4 1 9 2 7 *